LIGHT UP –

The Potential of Light in Museum Architecture

Edition Angewandte – Book series of
the University of Applied Arts Vienna
Edited by Gerald Bast, Rector

edition:'ʌngewʌndtə
Universität für angewandte Kunst Wien
University of Applied Arts Vienna

Andrea Graser

Light Up –

The Potential of Light in Museum Architecture

Birkhäuser
Basel

Contents

PROLOGUE

Whether one beholds the space where art is displayed or the art being displayed within, light is the common denominator.

The interrelationship between the arts, as well as two different perspectives regarding the use of light as a material in the exhibition space, forms the springboard for *Light Up – The Potential of Light in Museum Architecture.* As an architect, I examine the subject through an analytical approach to exhibition space and museum architecture. My perspective has been broadened by the insights of Friedrich Biedermann, an artist who uses light as a medium in his works.

Both of us studied at the University of Applied Arts Vienna and over the course of our long careers as architect and artist we have pursued this theme. Together, we developed a theory of the *object-oriented ontology of light*, which regards light as spiritual matter uniting the architectural space, the artwork and the viewer. Once one sees light as a material in the museum, then one can begin to assess its potential in the exhibition space. In galleries and art museums, our perception of art, space and atmosphere is essentially determined by lighting. This book begins by asking why lighting is simply taken for granted, regarded merely as a light source rather than as a creator of mood affecting our perception of an artwork, allowing us to view and interpret it in new ways.

Western society spends more than 80 percent of its time indoors in private and public spaces—mostly artificially illuminated. What is the character of these artificially lit spaces and how do we experience them? When measured with a digital spectrometer, the quality of illumination in a prestigious museum is hardly different to the light spectrum found inside a typical fast-food restaurant. Commercial businesses purposefully use lighting to manipulate specific consumer behavior. Can the same be said in the context of exhibition architecture? Our measurements of the lighting conditions in actual exhibition spaces have revealed remarkable disparities in light quality, raising questions about how art can convey different meaning under different lighting conditions.

The evolution of light sources and their relative lighting qualities over the past decades has shaped our perception of art. Perhaps it has impacted art itself. Could the popularity of acrylic paints in contemporary art be the result of the prevalent use of fluorescent lighting in exhibition spaces and artist studios during the 1980s? Today, pioneering LED technologies allow us to create customized lighting scenarios. Artificial light is becoming an interactive material in museum architecture, not only in terms of conceptual design but as real-time spatial experiences. Exploring the potential of dynamic artificial lighting technologies in museum architecture opens up new perspectives and approaches to the use of light in exhibition spaces. But how should art experts, museum professionals and exhibition designers decide upon which light settings to use?

One must understand darkness in order to work with light. Otherwise how can one isolate light and regard it separately from interpretation? How is one supposed to find the balance between awareness and interpretation? In the past we perceived natural light filtered through church windows, while today we behold the artificial light of our smartphones. From day one, we are exposed to and interpret light, which we take for granted and enjoy! Therefore, it is not so easy to differentiate light from perception! My approach begins with dark spaces. For me, light is an ongoing experiment that conveys evidence and existence, and it changes from day to day. Our primal instincts are imprinted within us. Wary of darkness, we turn to the light. Certain colors in nature signal danger. Light can have a calming or a compelling effect on us. All this information is stored in our DNA.

(Biedermann 2022)

▷ Figure 1. Measurement of the lighting conditions in actual exhibition spaces with a portable spectrometer
Artwork in background: Friedrich Biedermann, *I Have Seen Reality*, 2020

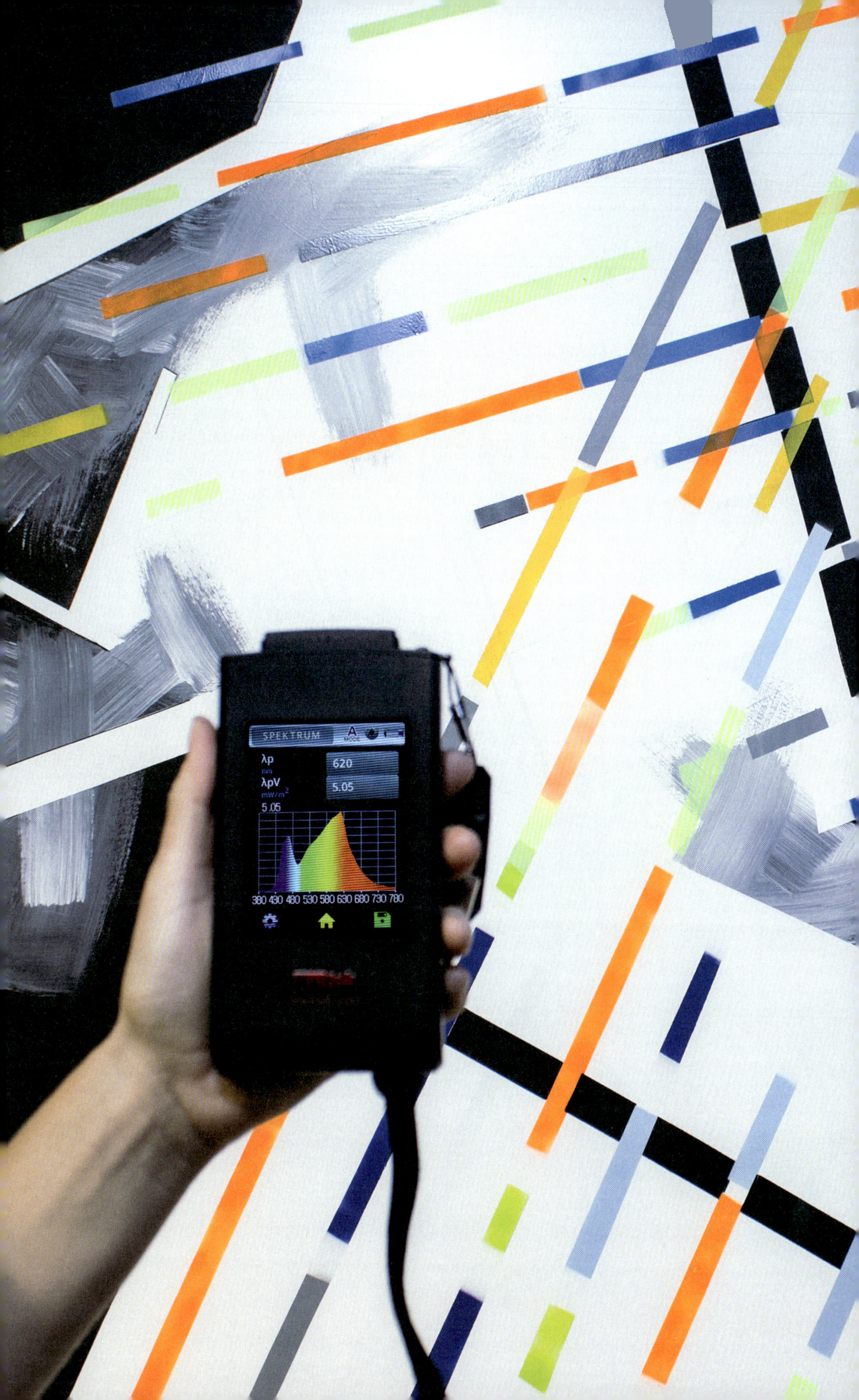
SPEKTRUM
A
λp
620
λpV
5.05
5.05
380 430 480 530 580 630 680 730 780

One should be able to change the heights and the widths of the rooms at will. If possible, automatically. Skylight, daylight from side, should be excluded. All in all, an ideal museum would be changeable to any size, and dimension, and the light, too.

(Kiesler 1966: 94)

Dynamic artificial lighting offers artists, architects, curators and museum experts nearly unlimited possibilities for illuminating an exhibition space. But how should the various nuances of artificial light interact with the artwork and the exhibition space? What potential does dynamic artificial lighting provide as an interactive material in galleries and art museums? What is the relationship between light and the artwork, exhibition space and audience? What happens to this relationship when lighting is implemented as an interactive tool? Can dynamic artificial lighting design be controlled within the exhibition space? What are the signature characteristics of contemporary lighting?

Digital measurement methods can be integrated with digital light sources making it possible to transfer lighting moods dynamically from one space to another. Just as it is possible to digitally scan an object, a room or a building and then plot it as a three-dimensional model, it is also possible to measure the light at a specific location using a digital spectrometer, store the data and reproduce it in a new environment using state-of-the-art lighting technology. It is thus theoretically possible to reproduce in the exhibition space the light under which a work of art was created in the studio. One could also reproduce the light used at New York City's Museum of Modern Art (MoMA) in Vienna's Museum of Modern and Contemporary Art (mumok). Taking this concept further, one might use digitally controlled dynamic lighting systems to travel in time—for example, from the light of the present day to that of the Baroque—or to transport the light of Central Europe to the light of the North or South. How might such possibilities impact museum lighting in the near future?

When one recognizes that light determines and shapes the appearance and perception of art and its exhibition spaces, one can see the potential of dynamic artificial lighting within galleries and art museums as an interactive material for artists, architects and curators. This was analyzed from an architect's standpoint—one that regards light as an environmental material—specifically, by evaluating whether dynamic artificial light sources can perfectly reproduce natural lighting conditions.

THE LIGHT OF OUR DAY

Light is a variable that allows us to interact with the space, the art and the audience in real time. Therefore, with regard to contemporary art, our goal as exhibition designers should be to create a contemporary exhibition space. This goal is based on the realization that our perception of art has always been shaped by prevailing artificial-lighting technology. Artificial light has become more relevant as museums have shunned natural light (for conservation reasons) and the white, neutralizing space has become the standard credo of exhibition architecture, whose main goal has been suppressing any distraction from the art itself. Because of this, over the past decades, our perception of art has depended upon the quality of the light sources applied in each case. It can be argued that lighting within the exhibition space has the potential to influence artistic developments: Might acrylic paint have gained prevalence because of fluorescent lighting? Dynamic artificial lighting could become an incubator allowing new art to develop, generating new freedoms in the creative process and the choice of materials. Light can now be dynamically harmonized with the art.

Dynamic lighting allows us to perceive art in all its facets. Our perception of an artwork can be altered by its illumination. Such changes can be induced deliberately and used as a design tool. In the process, the question of light's potential is directly related to the issue of the *light of our day*. Indeed, dynamic artificial lighting enables us to actively influence the established pattern of relationships in the here and now.

The findings of the White Cube Teleporter research project demonstrate that a dynamic artificial light source can disrupt the predominant patterns of relationships between exhibition space, art and the viewing public, thereby opening up new levels of perception. It has been shown that viewers' preferences for how art is illuminated vary considerably and do not directly correspond with the prevailing lighting we currently encounter in museums. In the first case study, we could ascertain that the audience preferred light with cool color temperatures for viewing early 20th-century portraits, and light with warm color temperatures for abstract contemporary art—a result at odds with the light settings prevalent in today's museums. Surveys of existing museums have shown us that we currently experience art under static light sources with a constant color temperature that varies depending on the illuminants used, and that contemporary art is primarily displayed under cool color temperatures, unlike historical paintings, which are typically viewed under a color temperature of around 2,700 Kelvin. As a dynamic changing light source, the sun plays an essential role in the development of our visual perception of objects and space, color and three-dimensionality. Accordingly, dynamic and changing light should be a basic need for viewing art.

Results from the White Cube Teleporter series of experiments indicate that light supports the dialogue between viewer and art and can be used deliberately as a filter. Light acts as a mediator between definition and diffusion. In this way, light delineated the contours of the portraits and defined the facial features more strongly. It altered the portrait subjects' facial complexion, thus altering how we associate their character traits. We could use light to change the perception of depth in abstract images, shifting the relationship between foreground and background. Dynamically changing the light settings brought out different details of image content and the pictures became animated. The lighting gave the process of viewing art an unexpected dynamism. Even though we were able to discover all these aspects in the course of our series of experiments, we were unable to provide empirical evidence that light can significantly influence our appreciation of art. Even though we have not yet succeeded in establishing evidence for this, I believe that light can actively change our perception of art.

Experience has shown that users of dynamic lighting systems are often overwhelmed by the manifold options available to them. Our expertise allows us to select customized presets for them. When it comes to the targeted implementation of dynamic artificial light sources, it is up to us to actively design lighting settings and lighting programs that ease the users' decision-making by limiting the available options. Therefore, for our above-mentioned testing, the selection was limited to five settings. Public viewers were given the ability to change these settings at will. The choice of program and especially the speed with which the selection was made, as well as the duration of each setting, varied greatly and obviously depended largely on each individual's personality. The diverse participants included both quick studies, who ran through the programmed lighting settings in rapid succession, and leisurely indulgers spending several minutes with each respective setting.

This finding confirmed my belief that the choice of dynamic light sources is a very individual one, dependent upon the personality, gender, age, experience and preferences of the expert. It would seem that there are too many options for correctly illuminating art. The flexibility inherent in designing and programming dynamic light sources makes the role of the expert in defining clear parameters all the more important.

But what parameters *are* defined by experts today? We have known since the interview series by Garside et al. (2017) that museum professionals value visual testing highly. In other words, they test and try out different settings on site. Illuminating an exhibition is thus a process, and each picture's lighting is individually configured. Even though the possibilities are limited by the prevailing light sources, this method could prove as effective when using dynamic light sources. We know that experts are familiar with lighting artwork and that they make the decisions about how this is done. However, almost all the studies available to us have shown us that there is a wide range of (often contradictory) variation in lighting techniques—for example, decisions about the ideal color temperature—showing us that the choices of each expert are quite subjective.

Guidelines, recommendations and prevailing opinions have been disseminated and influence how we light exhibition spaces; however, the fact remains that there are no universally accepted rules. Look no further than the accepted standard for illuminating light-sensitive artworks with a maximum illuminance value of 50 lux. This did not originate from any clear conservation guidelines, but was rather derived from a study by Thomson, which focused on visual preferences, not illuminance (cf. Thomson 1986: 25ff.). Nevertheless, this value was codified as early as the 1960s, and museum professionals remain loathe to stray from this dogma.

Neither the results of previous studies nor the results of our research provide a definitive answer as to what is the best lighting for art. Since there are as yet no generally applicable guidelines, we experts must define the best lighting for art. The process of harmonizing lighting with the artwork in an exhibition space is an ongoing work in progress. This was also the premise behind our research, in which we tried to block out existing recommendations and tap into the potential of dynamic light sources.

In the first series of experiments of the White Cube Teleporter research project, the audience viewed the art always under one fixed light setting, preset by us, which varied from one series of experiments to the next. The viewers' attention was focused on the art, not the lighting. In the course of this experiment, we were able to determine that the audience responds to the spatial conditions within the exhibition area and does not attribute any particular role to lighting as a fixed component of the space. It seems we take lighting conditions for granted and adapt to them uncritically. Our attention is primarily focused on the artwork when viewing an exhibition. In contrast to similar studies, our experiments were designed in such a way to emulate a *real* exhibition space, yielding experiences on par with actual exhibition visits. In doing so, we were able to produce a very natural and intuitive approach to the medium of light in the exhibition space.

Our second series of experiments was also conducted with an audience in an exhibition environment. The lighting was now set up in the space as a customizable tool and integrated into the exhibition experience. In doing so, we were able to raise the audience's awareness of how lighting impacts the viewing of art. We could thus explore the potential of dynamic artificial lighting together with the audience and examine more closely the question of the *light of our day*. Artworks by the five contemporary artists were selected to demonstrate the versatility of dynamic light sources, in dialogue with the audience. It was as if we—audience and artists—were together inventing a new language and thus it was primarily up to the willingness of the artists and the audience to adopt this language, or at least open themselves up to it. In this context, a completely new significance was attributed to exhibition lighting. Interestingly, this language could be used as an intermediator for all five of the exhibited artworks, yielding quite different results. The lighting acted as a filter; image animator; narrator; enhancer of contrast and color; and it could soften or sharpen contours.

In this second series of experiments taking place in the exhibition *Five Artists × Five Museums*, the audience engaged with the lighting in two distinct ways: For one, an automated dynamic lighting system was used, in which the light settings changed automatically at fixed time intervals; for the other, the audience took on the active role of a stage director and could individually choose the light settings (from presets we designed) for each artwork at the push of a button. That all five artworks in one exhibition room were lit differently did not cause any irritation among the audience in the course of Case Study 02.

Driven to answer the question: "What is the *light of our day*?" our third series of experiments cast lighting as the lead actor in the stage play of exhibition space, art and audience. This experiment was all about discarding previous approaches and charting new territory. What happens when dynamic lighting takes the leading role in creating the audience's perception of change in the exhibition space, and thereby giving the art an interactive framework? In this way, the lighting could both complement and dissociate itself from both the art and the individual preferences of the audience. This generated both moments of pleasure and irritation, yet offered us myriad opportunities to perceive art and the experience of art. If we accept that there is no right or wrong with regard to lighting, and that a subjective and impulsive decision-making process lies behind one's opinion of art illumination (as it does for one's opinions of artworks), then we can see how the possibility of changing lighting during our exhibition visit, allowing us a variety of perspectives, corresponds fittingly to our zeitgeist. In the course of our *Lighthouse* experiment, the potential for dynamic artificial lighting as interactive material in gallery space became apparent. It can alter the way we look at art and reveal new levels of perception that are not possible in exhibition spaces with static artificial lighting conditions.

The experiment also demonstrated that lighting, as a unifying element, weaves together art and space. In other words, by tailoring the lighting to the art, the art becomes part of the exhibition space, and the audience is situated within this pattern of relationships. I view this pattern of relationships in relation to the concept of object-oriented ontology, in which the essence of objects is defined as their real and sensual qualities and their dependencies on each other, thus re-contextualizing light as a material (as an object in space).

▷ Figure 2. Friedrich Biedermann, *Light Path*, 2016, photo (detail) of light installation, Frankfurt am Main, Germany

THE ONTOLOGY OF LIGHT— RETHINKING LIGHT AS A MATERIAL

Ever since we created the concept, space has held whatever we put into it. We have imagined space to be many things, and that act of imagination has had implications for our image of light. Endow space with divinity and light is godlike; discover its shape and light is geometrical; fill it with matter and light is substantial. From Moses to Einstein, the history of light is also the history of space.

(Zajonc 1993: 97)

As an architectural material, light shapes our experience of space and object—of the White Cube (see page 46) and the art displayed within. This pertains not only to visual perception, which is inherently defined by light and shadow, but also to nonvisual perception, which is not generally associated with light. However, if one considers the theories of object-oriented ontology (OOO) and assumes that everything in this world is either a potential object, a potential pattern of relationships, or a form (cf. Haun 2002: 347–365), light can be contextualized in the exhibition space and characterized within a pattern of relationships. According to OOO, associations depend mainly on relationship patterns, which in turn are comprised of objects and qualities.

When a painting is hung on a wall, a relationship pattern has been established between two things—the painting and the exhibition wall. As soon as one becomes aware of the presence of light in the space, it too becomes connected with the space-forming elements of the White Cube, the art displayed within it, and the viewing audience. The light instantly becomes part of the relationship patterns (see fig. 3).

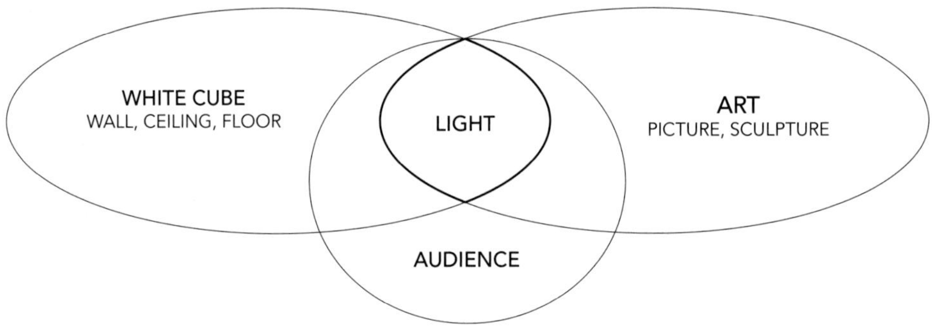

△ Figure 3. Diagram: relationship patterns between light, White Cube, art, audience

If one conceives of light as matter, in the sense of OOO, one could also characterize light with the traits of an object. Regarding an object, we distinguish between its real qualities and sensual qualities (cf. Harman 2018: 79f.). The real substance of light is its physical describability. It also possesses sensual qualities that only gain significance within a pattern of relationships.

We have arrived at a time where it is becoming possible, with the help of artificial light sources, to bring the sun indoors. At least since the Gothic era, daylight has been valued as a design element. But what about artificial lighting? Until now, it was not possible to replicate daylight, so deployment of indoor light sources has been limited to static parameters. As it is now possible to bring dynamic, variable light into the room, there is no getting around dealing with the essential nature of light. Today, we have virtually unlimited possibilities for producing artificial light. As soon as one comprehends the effective impact of artificial lighting, a desired result can be targeted by selecting and applying the proper lighting technique and controls.

For millennia, the question "What is light?" has preoccupied scientists, philosophers, theologists, artists and engineers, who have posited many theories. The first scientific findings on light are attributed to Alhazen (Ibn al-Haytham, c. 965–1040 AD, Cairo) and are outlined in his *Book of Optics* (cf. Verma 1969: 12ff.). Today's scientific knowledge of light is based largely on the corpuscular theory of Isaac Newton (c. 1700) and on the wave theory, as confirmed by Thomas Young's double-slit experiment (1802). Einstein (1905) finally defined light by what it is: both wave *and* particle.

> **In short, the young Einstein recognized the dual nature of light, and he remained astonished at this revolutionary insight as long as he lived, for his science had suddenly lost something very important, namely the ability to provide clear explanations and definitive solutions. (…) Since Einstein's time, light—viewed in the clear light of day—has been a mystery, and that is perhaps the best thing that could have happened to him (and us).**
>
> (Bachmann, Fischer 2006: 92)

In trying to understand light as an architectural material, I have come to appreciate the term "ontology of light," as this concept allows one to describe light's qualities by more than its mere physical characteristics. Just as a three-dimensional object in space can have a relationship to the space and the other objects located there, light also gains significance only in relation to its surroundings. Light's interaction with the space, the artworks and the viewers make it what it is.

The moment the light is turned on, the exhibition space, the art and the people within form an apparent relationship. Light becomes the unifying element. Light only becomes visible to us when we perceive its reflection off matter. The walls, the floor, the ceiling, the art and the visitors are only connected by means of light. Thus, it is the existence of light that defines our presence in the space relative to the White Cube and the art.

THE REAL QUALITIES OF LIGHT—A VIEW OF THE RELATIONSHIP BETWEEN LIGHT, ART AND ARCHITECTURE

I have always been fascinated by the hidden, essential nature of the material light, when it is applied to creating architecture and space—space that is perceived in its own right and that merges synergistically with constructed volumes and objects. It is the appearance of light that fascinates me—the atmospheric experience that can only result from the interaction of light and architecture. My focus is on artificial light sources that replicate sunlight and allow all facets of dynamic light to be brought into the space.

Light has the potential to be sensed as space. A streetlight, for example, is perceived as a cone of light in the darkness. Light can also appear as forms of natural phenomena. We are all familiar with the image of sunbeams breaking through the clouds or radiating across a Gothic church's nave—such examples help us to comprehend light as a material and allow it to be understood as an architectural construct. When it comes to my work with light, I usually explain it in the following way:

> **Light is material, and I use this material to design sculptures, objects and architecture. You can say I use 30,000 tons of steel, but you can also say I use 30,000 tons of light. In the end, it's the symbiosis—but I imagine space as a light space first and not the other way around.**
>
> (Graser 2017)

Even if one conceives of light as an architectural material in its own right, in the end it is invariably about light coexisting with space, which is especially true when it comes to museum architecture. Consider, for example, the Louvre in Abu Dhabi by Jean Nouvel, the Städel Museum in Frankfurt am Main by Schneider+Schumacher, the Broad Museum in Los Angeles by Diller Scofidio, or the Kunsthaus in Bregenz by Peter Zumthor—to name only a few art museums where light plays a leading role in the overall architectural concept.

Use of dynamic lighting in interiors could engender a new perspective of light. To accomplish this, we have to come to terms with our current understanding of light and seek to interpret it as architecture. Frederick Kiesler's 1942 Art of This Century gallery in New York sought to convey the expressive zeitgeist of his era through the space's lighting (cf. Davis 2005: 207ff.)—a goal to which we, too, should aspire today in using light as a design tool in contemporary exhibition spaces. Dynamic artificial light sources enable us to express aspects of the *light of our day*. It is necessary for us to discover and understand light in the here and now. To do this, architects and artists must consider new strategies for light within the creative process and adopt dynamic lighting technologies as a design medium.

The development of a new creative approach to lighting can be compared to the way the original dynamic light source—sunlight—became a spatial design tool in the early 12th century. The design process of a Gothic cathedral was governed by the influence of light (e.g., Basilica of Saint-Denis, north of Paris). In the Baroque era, artists such as Michelangelo Merisi da Caravaggio (1571–1610) experimented with direct natural light sources to execute *chiaroscuro* (starkly contrasted light and shadow) painting technique, starting a conscious trend toward painting in natural light as opposed to candlelight. Caravaggio's paintings provide a great example of the interplay between painted light and the light that illuminates the painting within the exhibition space. This became apparent to me while viewing Caravaggio's *The Crowning with Thorns* at Vienna's Kunsthistorisches Museum during its exhibition *Caravaggio and Bernini* (exhibition period: 15 October 2019–19 January 2020). The painting is in the museum's permanent collection and is normally displayed in its Picture Gallery, so it had already been part of my lighting measurements in January 2018.

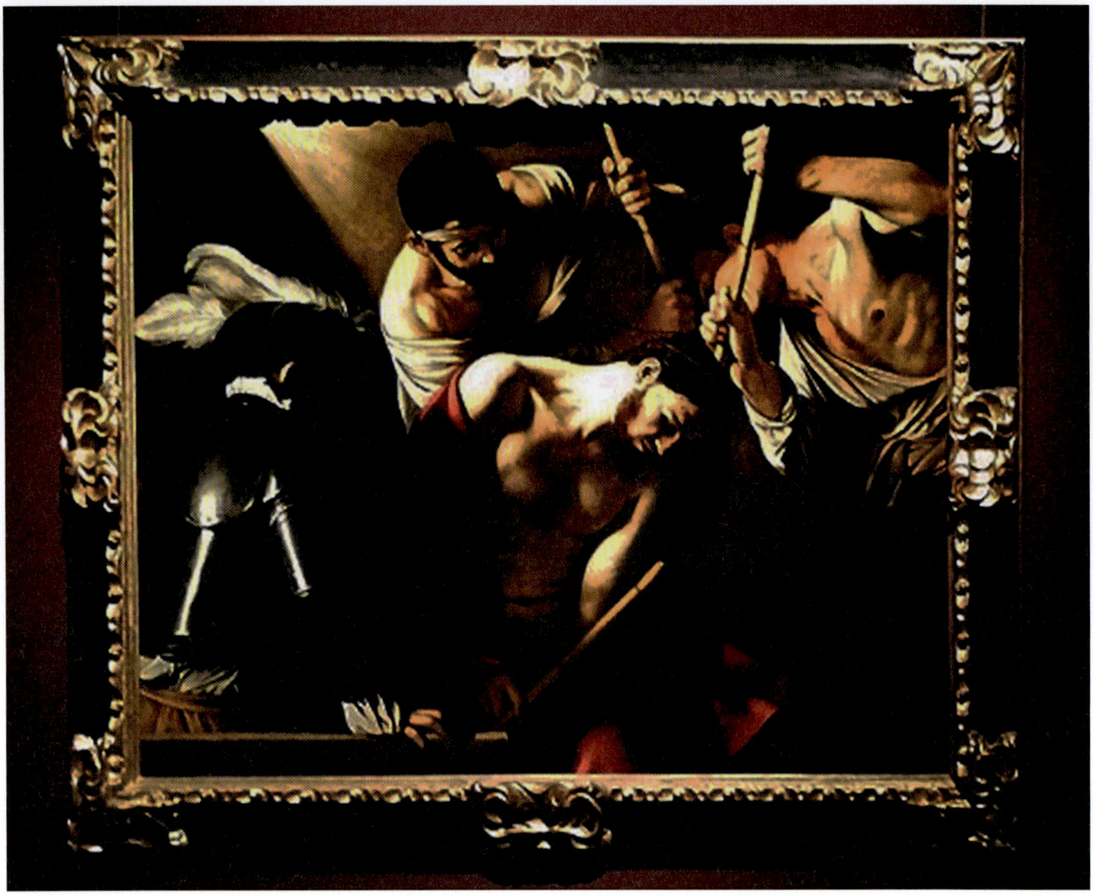

△ Figure 4. Photo taken 18 January 2018, *The Crowning with Thorns* by Michelangelo Merisi da Caravaggio (c. 1601), KHM Vienna, Picture Gallery, permanent exhibition, Room VI

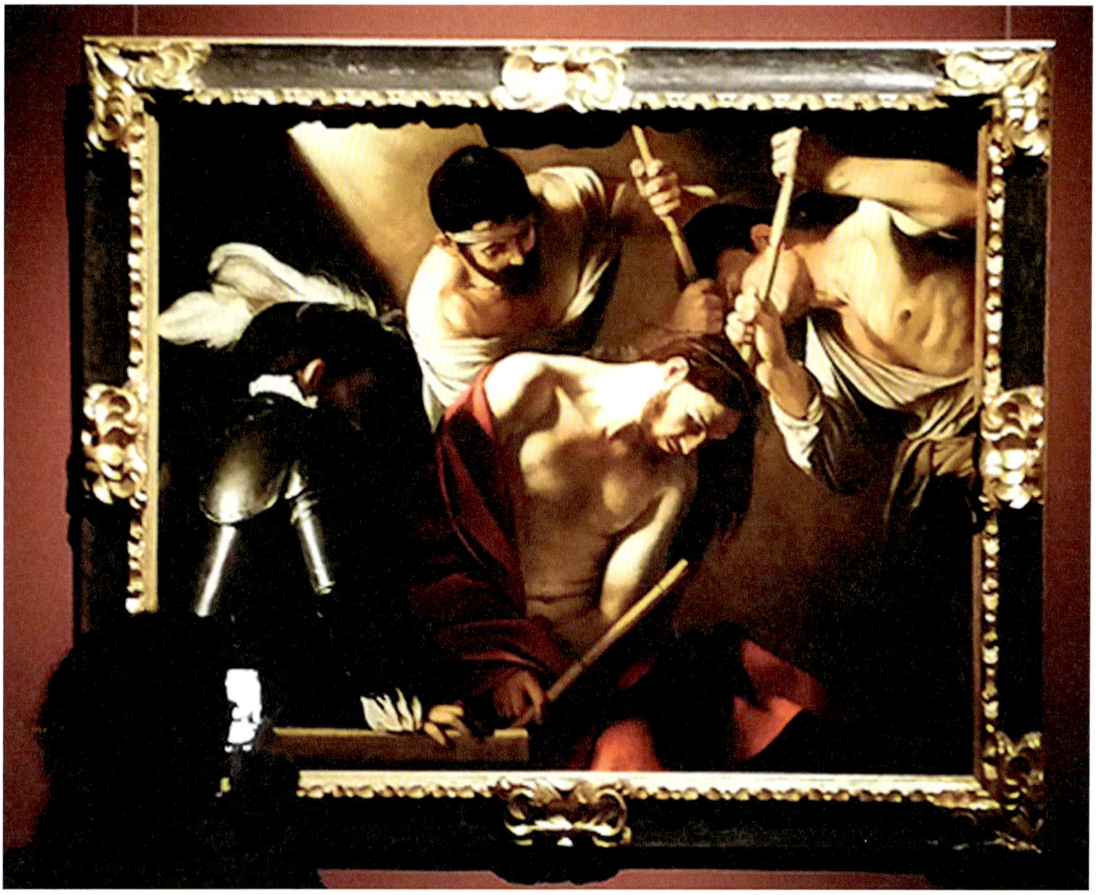

△ Figure 5. Photo taken 13 January 2020, *The Crowning with Thorns* by Michelangelo Merisi da Caravaggio (c. 1601), KHM Vienna, special exhibition *Caravaggio and Bernini*, Room IV

The juxtaposition of the photos from my documentation illustrates how the visual perception of the painting is affected by its illumination (see figs. 4–5). The full power of the painting in all its facets was on view during the special exhibition—the light depicted in the painting radiated beyond its gilded frame into the exhibition. This perceptual experience renewed my resolve to confront the issue of the light of our zeitgeist. The use of a new generation of museum spotlights gives us a sense of the potential that lies within future lighting technologies. Where will awareness of the subject of light lead us in this day and age, if we bring together contemporary art with forward-looking technologies and sciences?

Although electric light had been around since the mid-19th century, artistic research with artificial light did not begin until 1937, with László Moholy-Nagy's founding of the New Bauhaus in Chicago. It described itself as an institution where art, science and technology merged in a creative network "[...] to form a nucleus for an independent reliable educational center, where art, science, technology will be united to a creative pattern." (Karasov 1995: 13). It is the time when artificial light first defines stage scenery and becomes part of artistic experiments. The first light sculptures are also created.

Artists such as James Turrell, Robert Irwin and Douglas Wheeler also began to develop their work in the field of light by conducting experimental, scientific and art-based happenings as part of the Los Angeles [California] County Museum of Art's *Art and Technology Program*, established in 1967–78 by the curator Maurice Tuchman (cf. Tuchman 1971). In Europe, around the same time, there were a handful of artists in Paris (Nicolas Schöffer and the group GRAV) and the German group ZERO (Otto Piene, Heinz Mack), who experimented with light art, light objects and visual perception. They all established a fundamental understanding of *light as material* in art, which also paved the way for a new generation of light artists, such as Mischa Kuball and Olafur Eliasson.

Our own projects are also characterized by a merging of art, technology and science. *Light Path*, for example, is a mobile art installation created in cooperation with the artist Friedrich Biedermann and the Lumitech company's research and development department, and was first exhibited at the *Luminale 2016* in Frankfurt am Main (see fig. 6). The installation is built inside the cargo bay of a truck. When the tailgate is opened, the audience is invited to enter the space inside, which is lined with a translucent material that diffuses artificial light (invisibly installed and dynamically controlled by a program). The real flow of natural light is simulated—day and night elapse in just two minutes. No matter where and when the truck stops, its visitors experience a two-minute light shower, in time lapse.

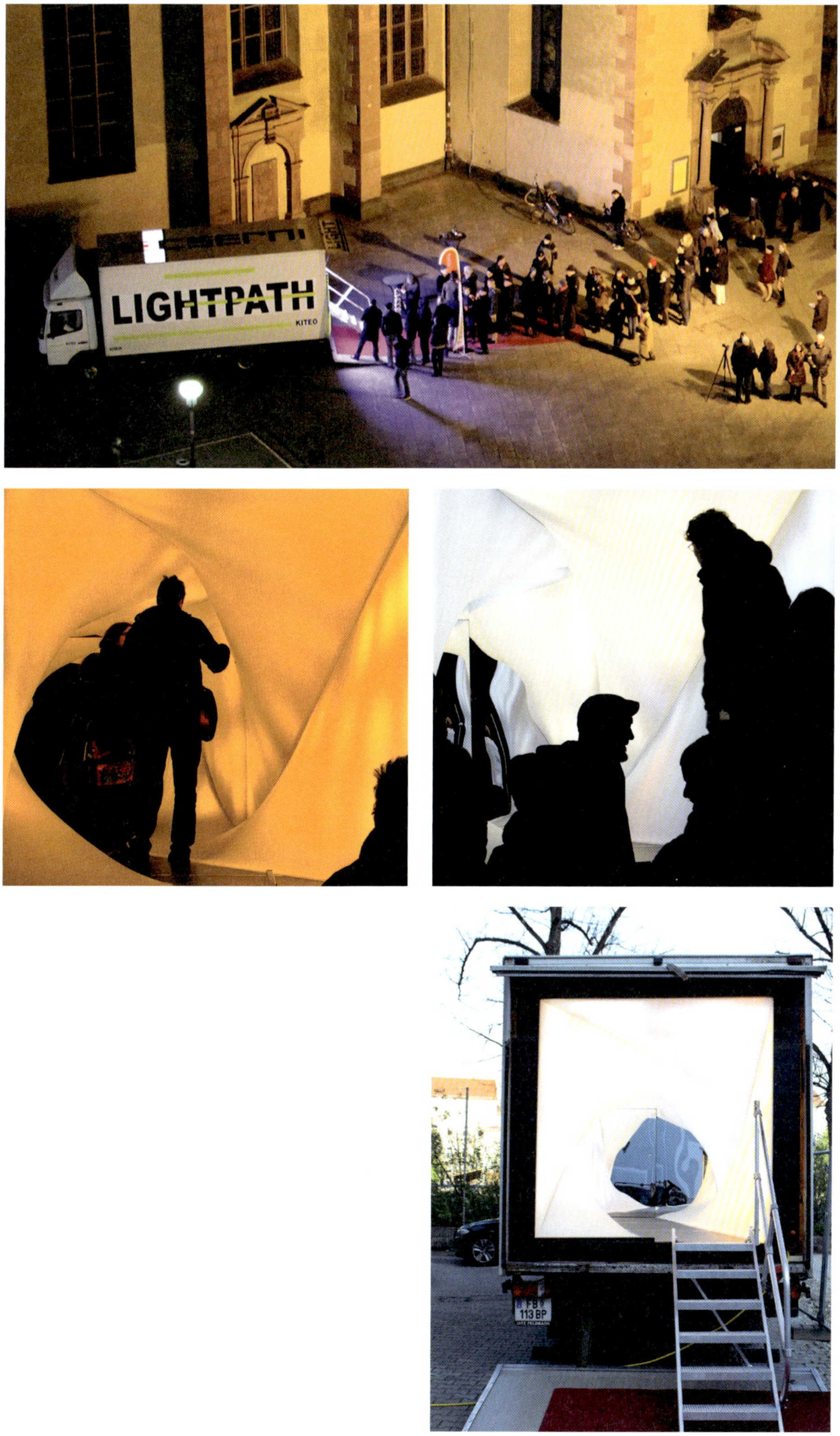

△▷ Figure 6. Photo gallery of light installation by Friedrich Biedermann, *Light Path*, 2016, Frankfurt am Main, Germany

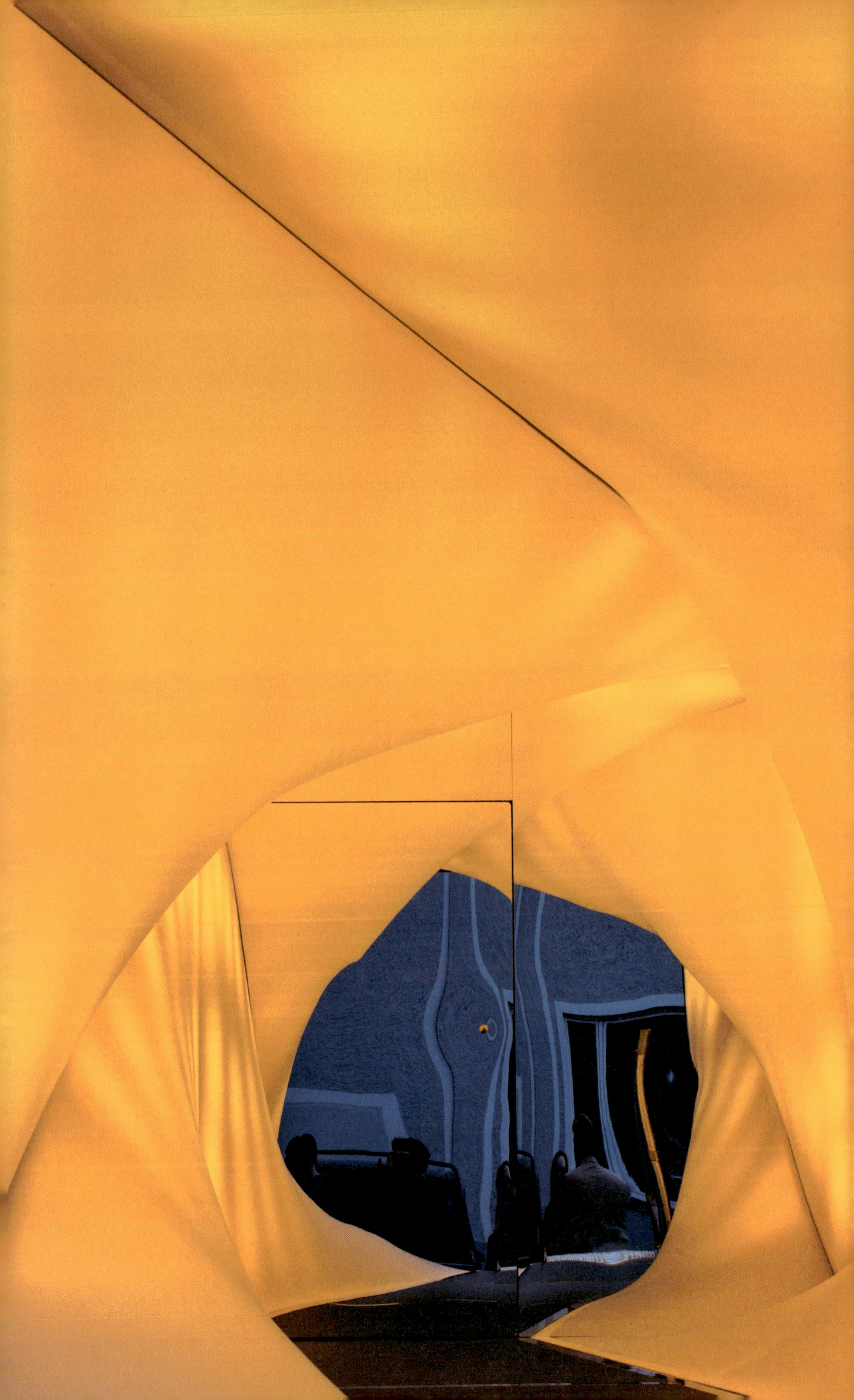

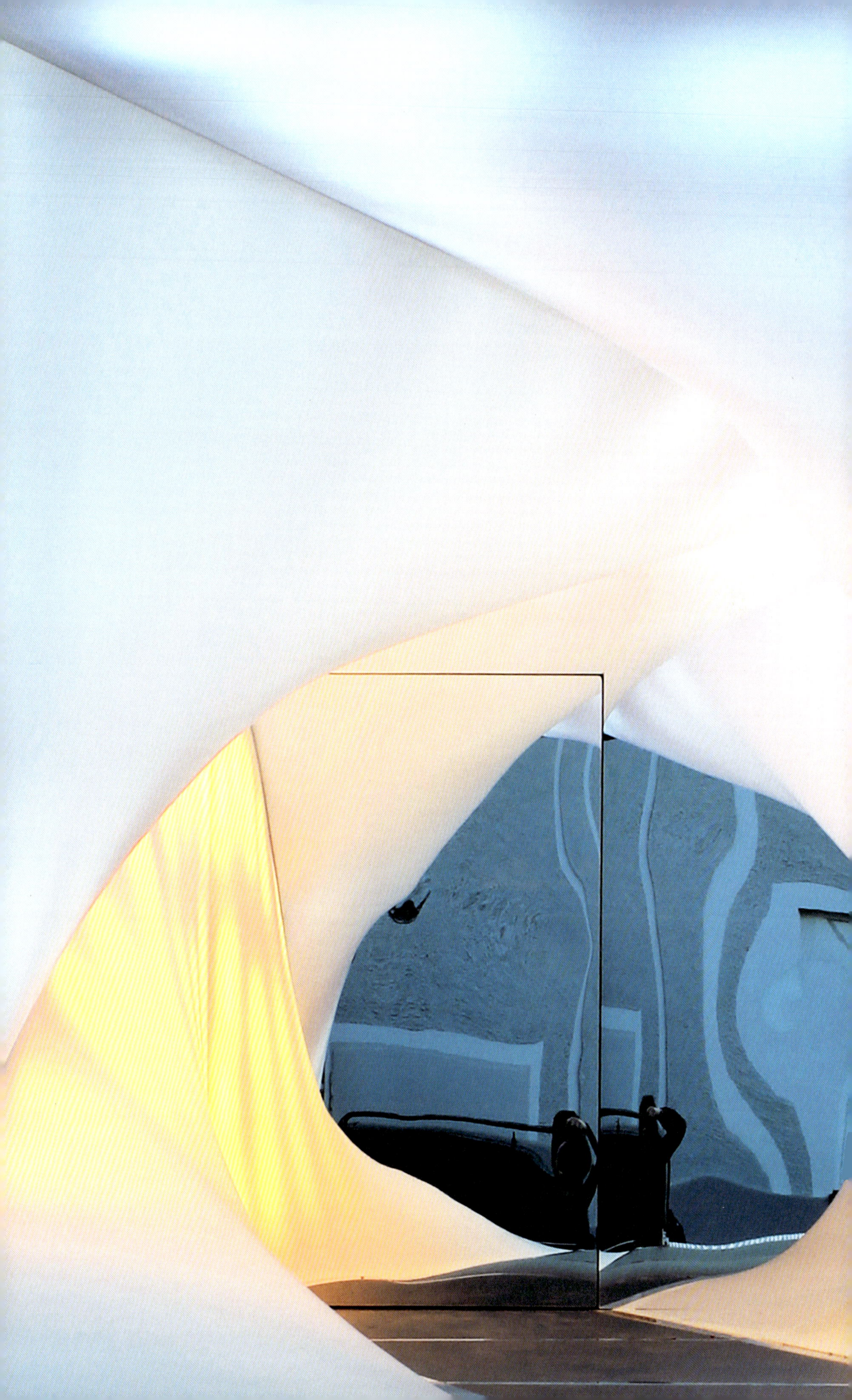

THE SENSUAL QUALITIES OF LIGHT— EXAMINING THE PATTERN OF RELATIONSHIPS BETWEEN LIGHT AND SPACE

Our understandings of light are thus entwined with our conceptions of space. They have coevolved: moral space and spiritual light, perspective space and geometrical light, material space and substantial light. Each age emphasized one face of light and so revealed its own predilections.

(Zajonc 1993: 99)

Light is a fascinating subject. If one speaks of light as a material, one simply cannot explain its nature using only mathematical and physical laws. Scientific insights and discoveries form the basis for approaching the topic and then for working out the specifics for how dynamic artificial lighting can qualitatively simulate natural light. However, the question of the *essence* of light remains. This insight has become increasingly important to me, especially in the course of conducting our White Cube experiments.

When we enter a museum, we become immersed in a certain ambience that establishes our perception of the surroundings and the architectural environment.

In the context of Gothic church interiors, such ambiance is generated almost exclusively by light, such as in Abbot Suger's reconstruction of the Basilica of Saint-Denis, located north of Paris. The beauty of this context is that light can reveal its true nature before it undergoes manipulation or modification. That is to say, the light itself—its natural color, its changing intensity and the dynamic flow of daylight—is used as a design tool to create the space's atmosphere. This is basically how artificial lighting is defined within the contemporary field of Human Centric Lighting: pure white light, whose changing color temperature and intensity are modeled on natural sunlight, mimicking its spectrum and attempting to reproduce daylight in all its nuances.

While the Gothic period architecture appreciated light for its purity, Baroque architecture casts it in an interplay of form, color and material—a role that we now associate with the term "effect lighting." Baroque light no longer appears exclusively in its natural purity, but is applied in combination with filters and reflectors, such as colorful stained-glass windows that transform the pervasive daylight. Three-dimensional forms create spatial shadow plays and the color gold takes on high importance. The so-called "Golden Hour" in Vienna's Jesuitenkirche affords a very impressive example of this. During the summer months, the sinking rays of the setting sun bathe Andrea Pozzo's 1702 baroque church interior in sublime evening light, illuminating the heavily gilt space in all its glory. As the sun sets, its rays slowly traverse the interior, allowing us to experience the space dynamically, almost as though one were witnessing a three-dimensional computer animation. The three-dimensional, moving imagery shapes our spatial experience.

Today, our relationship to light has changed significantly. Never before has lighting been more integrated into our lives. We are constantly immersed in it. We spend hours in front of our computer screens or smartphones. Virtual imagery shapes our perception of light, color and space in a way that has never been experienced before. As our visual perception is based on the processing of experiences, our understanding of light changes daily. For example, it is interesting to observe how colors in movies and animation disappear as the imagery in these media has become paler and more monochromatic. Do we long for a certain purism within the flood of visual imagery? Might our responsibility in handling dynamic light sources be counteracting visual overstimulation? Is this the zeitgeist of the *light of our day*?

[Each space] has its own character that impinges on us and takes hold of our feelings so that it falls into accord with this mood.

(Bollnow 1963: 234)

When you enter an art museum, it is one of those moments when you feel as if the pause button has been pressed and the experience of the space and discovery of the artworks are solely yours. Although museums are public buildings, usually well attended, this magic prevails and, I suggest, it is the atmosphere of the building and exhibition space that surrounds and captivates us. It creates a space that engages us and makes us recognize that we are in a unique place. Typically, one takes one's time to visit a museum and opens oneself up to the art. Consciously or not, we allow the site, the space and the architecture to affect us. According to Bollnow (cf. Bollnow 1963: 229ff.), each space has its own mood and he ascribes this to the atmospheric conditions.

Primarily concerned with visible space, Bollnow's categorization of day and night space could be compared to the findings of research into light's impact on the day-night cycle, the so-called circadian rhythm, which essentially shows that our perception of day and night also takes place on a nonvisual level. Several recent studies address the impact of artificial light on our biorhythms, well-being and behavior (cf. Chew et al. 2016; Hertog et al. 2015; Llenas and Carreras 2019; Llenas et al. 2019). Behavioral studies in workplaces, schools and clinics reveal the connections between dynamic lighting controls and mood, well-being, visual comfort and day-night rhythms. In the museum, not only the perfect illumination of art, but also the experience of art plays a major role. We feel emotions when we view art. If we recognize that light also influences our well-being, then we can conclude that the lighting of art also influences our emotions. So, one should focus on new technical achievements and scientific findings in lighting research (cf. Hurlbert et al. 2020). After all, the *experience* of art plays a key role in its interpretation.

HOW ARTIFICIAL LIGHTING AND ART MUSEUMS INTERACT

The concept that the essence of light transforms the mutable form of the exhibition space is based upon the premise that light is matter, in the sense of object-oriented ontology, and this is at the core of the web of relationships between art, exhibition space, and audience (see fig. 3, page 24).

If we focus on the two parameters of *artificial lighting* and *exhibition space*, we discover historical dependencies that have been influenced by technological developments and knowledge. Because natural daylight has a high potential for causing damage to artworks, the use of artificial light sources in the museum context plays a special role. The development of the art museum and the technical advances of artificial light sources have progressed hand in hand through the decades. The history of the art museum begins almost simultaneously with the invention of artificial light—specifically, the carbon filament lightbulb around 1880, which marked the onset of electrification.

HISTORICAL DEVELOPMENT OF ARTIFICIAL LIGHTING IN ART MUSEUMS

The dawning era of the art museum is said to have occurred between 1830 and 1880. The fact that electrification was not always a standard for museum design can be demonstrated by Vienna's Kunsthistorisches Museum (Museum of Art History, or KHM).

The KHM was built during the years 1871 to 1877. Its architects, Carl von Hasenauer and Gottfried Semper, planned it as a daylight museum, using skylights for illumination, which was common internationally ever since the Louvre's Grande Galerie was built in 1800. In Vienna, however, it was a somewhat controversial technique at the time, because until the construction of the Künstlerhaus in Vienna (1865–1870), paintings were commonly side-lit (such as in cabinets of curiosities, so-called *Wunderkammern*).

Since supplemental artificial lighting (e.g., gas lamps) was entirely omitted, the museum was only open during daytime—its visiting hours seasonally adjusted, accordingly. The basic electrification of the KHM was first implemented 100 years later in the galleries displaying the collections of Egyptian, oriental and Classical antiquities, and was finally completed in 2005, with the reopening of its *Kunstkammer*. Due to the damaging effect of daylight's ultraviolet rays on the paintings, all skylights were veiled and retrofitted with artificial lighting, as they were in so many other museums. Initially, fluorescent lamps were installed behind the glass ceilings—today, lighting of paintings is augmented by track spotlights. With the installation of static light sources, the building was robbed of its essential character, from an architectural point of view. For decades now, it has also deprived the viewer the possibility for viewing diverse paintings under different lighting conditions.

The lighting of exhibition spaces has long depended upon the quality of static artificial light sources. Couldn't these be replaced with LEDs that can emulate daylight? The lighting designer Veronika Mayerböck obviously thought so. Based on her designs, since 2019 the fluorescent tubes in the museum's glass ceilings have been gradually replaced by three channel LEDs and dynamically controlled. The passage of daylight diffused through skylights is simulated.

The KHM's exhibition walls are color-tinted and the exhibition architecture embodies a certain zeitgeist, apropos of its function as an art-history museum. That exhibition styles can develop in parallel with art movements is also evident in the development of the White Cube.

HISTORY OF THE WHITE CUBE

In 1883, the Fine Art Society of London presented an exhibition of the artist James McNeill Whistler in a gallery designed exclusively in yellow and white. The prints were framed in white and hung on a white background. According to Brown (cf. Brown 2018), this could mark the onset of the White Cube.

Ultimately, it was the Modern Art movement that elevated the White Cube exhibition style, mainly because groups such as Bauhaus or De Stijl in the 1920s insisted upon white walls for displaying their abstract art.

The White Cube follows the concept of displaying art in a white space in order to clearly emphasize the art over the exhibition architecture. One of the first museums to adopt this concept as standard practice was New York City's Museum of Modern Art (MoMA), which opened in 1939. The building's design was described as commercial, as opposed to monumental. In MoMA's exhibition spaces, the viewer's attention is focused on the art rather than the architecture (cf. Cain 2016). Around the same time (1942), Peggy Guggenheim opened her Art of This Century gallery in New York. Together with the architect Frederick Kiesler, she developed a completely new style of exhibition architecture for contemporary art.

Ever since the 1950s, the White Cube has become established as the predominant type of exhibition space. In the 1970s, it was theorized in terms of its central role as a neutral, white gallery space for exhibiting modernist art (cf. O'Doherty 1976/1986: 7ff.) and thus became further cemented into the consciousness of curators and exhibition designers. There were also artists who adopted the White Cube's aesthetics as a theme in and of itself: the artist Yves Klein turned an empty space into a work of art for his 1958 exhibition at the Iris Clert Gallery in Paris, entitled *Le vide* (The Void).

He placed a white display cabinet in the otherwise empty, white-washed space. The exterior window of the gallery was painted blue, a large blue theater curtain was hung in the entrance lobby, and the attendees at the exhibit's opening were served blue cocktails (cf. Cabañas 2008: pages 6–31).

Even today, there are many critical opinions in the art world when it comes to the White Cube. Still, the dominant popular opinion is that art is taken out of context by aestheticization and thus its (social) effect is neutralized.

If we now consider a White Cube in connection with light, it is ideally a white, windowless room illuminated artificially. These requirements are based on the well-worn concept of creating a space for art that is as neutral as possible—a space that does not distract from the art, in the spirit of Brian O'Doherty:

> **A gallery is constructed along laws as rigorous as those for building a medieval church. The outside world must not come in, so windows are usually sealed off. Walls are painted white. The ceiling becomes the source of light. The wooden floor is polished so that you click along clinically, or carpeted so that you pad soundlessly, resting the feet while the eyes have [*sic*] at the wall. The art is free as the saying used to go, "to take on its own life." (…) Unshadowed, white, clean, artificial—the space is devoted to the technology of esthetics.**
>
> (O'Doherty 1976/1986: 15)

O'Doherty maintains that the White Cube should be lit exclusively with artificial light, if possible. But he does not elaborate on any qualitative criteria for artificial light, nor on any specific requirements for lighting an exhibition space.

ARTIFICIAL LIGHT—A MATTER OF ZEITGEIST

Much discussion and debate surround the 20th-century White Cube exhibition space. Interestingly enough, however, there is very little information regarding artificial lighting for the White Cube. Numerous galleries are equipped with ceiling lamps. Quite often fluorescent lamps were used in White Cubes. The impact of lighting on exhibition spaces could also have a significant impact on art itself. I would even contend that acrylic paint gained favor among artists because its colors appear brighter under fluorescent lighting—and this hypothesis is largely accepted by curators and artists. Oils, on the other hand, appear especially impressive under candlelight or daylight. It could be inferred that artists, consciously or not, adapt their work to the lighting situation in studios and exhibition spaces. These observations reinforce my hypothesis that high-quality dynamic artificial light sources could have an impact on art.

As early as the 1940s, Frederick Kiesler realized that the contemporary zeitgeist could be incorporated into exhibition lighting of contemporary art. For Peggy Guggenheim's Art of This Century gallery in New York, for example, Kiesler not only conceived an unprecedented form of exhibition architecture—one forming a dialogue with the displayed art—but he illuminated the art in a unique way. In a press release from 20 October 1942 pertaining to the *Architectural Aspects of the Gallery*, Kiesler described his lighting concept as follows:

> **Improvements in lighting have been attempted especially in one of the permanent galleries where the indirect lighting can be controlled for each painting individually. In all galleries, however, the color, intensity and diffusion of light have been correlated in a new manner, namely, by planning the reflection coefficient of all the surfaces of the room in color as well as in volume and their combined effect upon paintings.**

(Kiesler 1942)

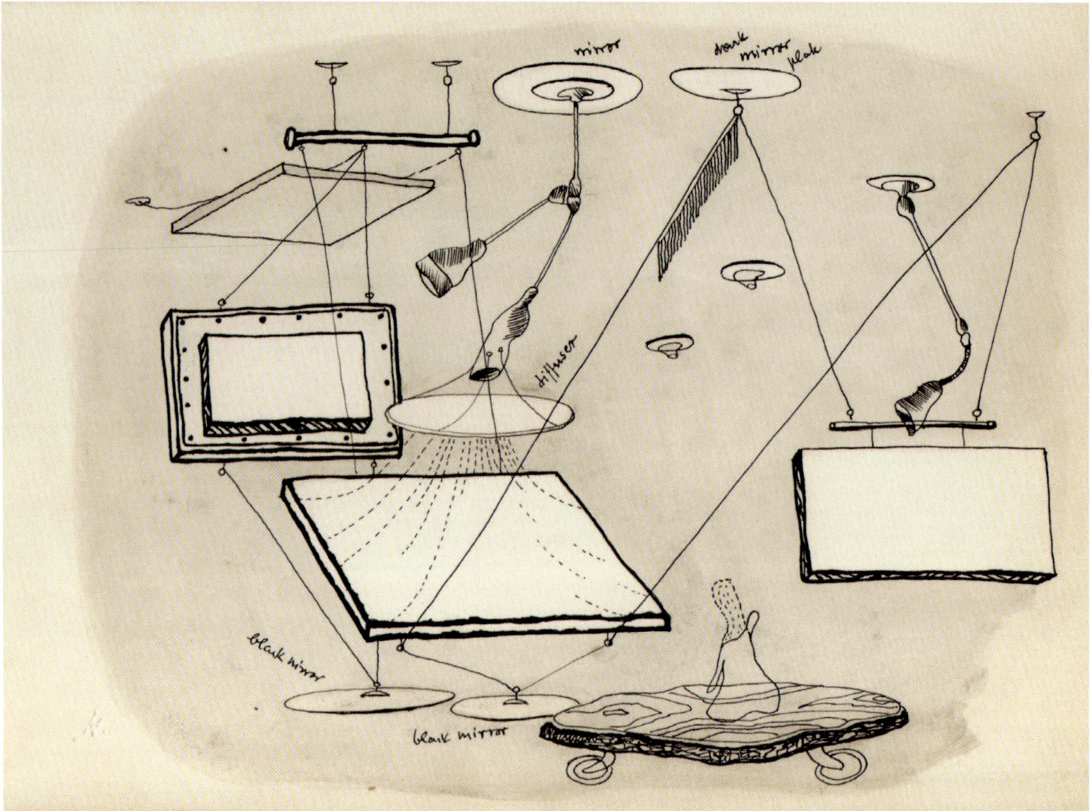

△ Figure 7. Frederick Kiesler, "Study for installing and lighting artworks in the 'Abstract Gallery,' New York," 1942, ink on paperboard, 8" × 11", © 2023 Austrian Frederick and Lillian Kiesler Private Foundation, Vienna

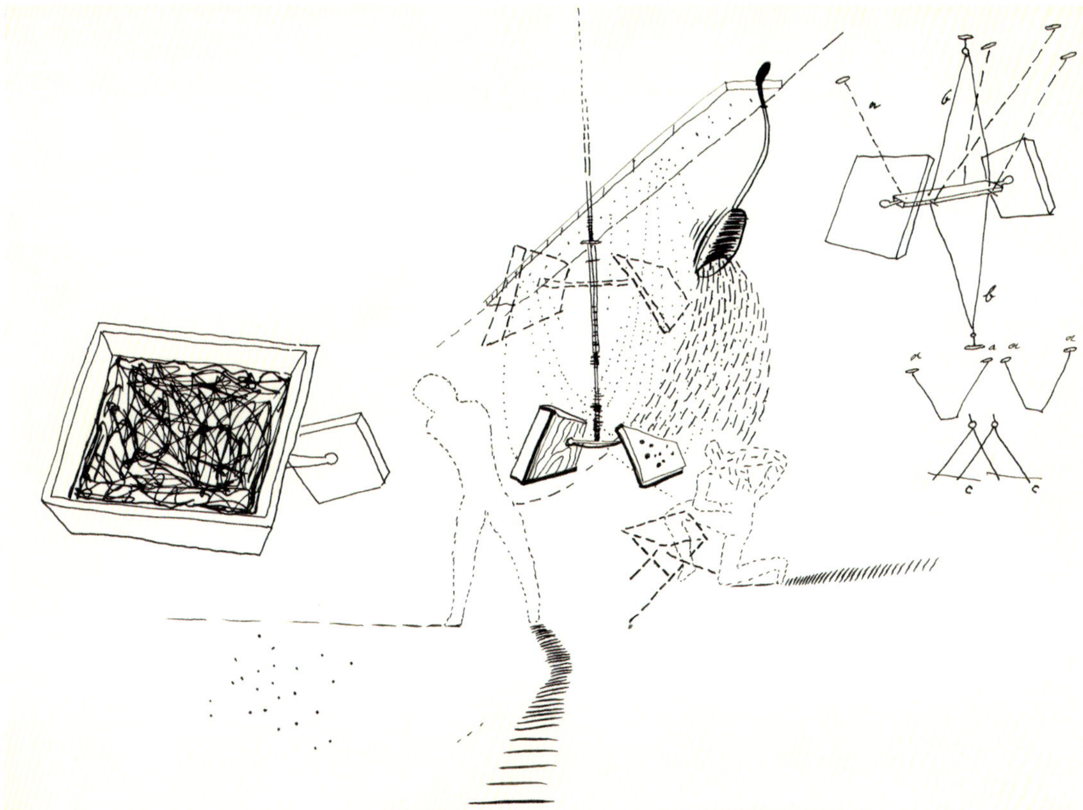

△ Figure 8. Frederick Kiesler, "Study for viewing artwork installed with an adjustable hanging method, New York," 1942, ink on paperboard, 8" × 11", © 2023 Austrian Frederick and Lillian Kiesler Private Foundation, Vienna

The Art of This Century gallery consisted of four areas: an "Abstract Gallery," a "Surrealist Gallery," a "Daylight Gallery" and a small "Kinetic Gallery." In the Abstract Gallery, the existing skylights were completely covered to block out daylight and fluorescent tubes were placed on a ceiling-mounted truss. One such lighting system was on display at the 1938 New York World's Fair and was used by architect William Muschenheim for the Museum of Non-Objective Painting. In the Surrealist Gallery, the pictures were lit individually with adjustable spotlights. Kiesler's sketches corroborate his thinking on how light sources should be oriented to the artwork and to the viewer, and prove that Kiesler thought of light as an interactive architectural material in space.

I see the lighting concept at Munich's Lenbachhaus art museum, which opened in 2013, as representing a comparable approach in our own day and age. Here, the architectural firm Foster + Partners, together with the engineering firm Ingenieure Bamberger GmbH & Co, implemented the illumination concept of the light artist Dietmar Tanterl. Their focus here was on using artificial illumination both to simulate daylight and to tailor lighting for each individual artwork. The lighting mood can be set for each individual room, in accordance with the exhibition. The implementation seems quite costly—as each setting requires a different spotlight, they had to install a disproportionate number of luminaires. Evidently, at that time they had not yet deployed Tunable White LED lighting controllers, with which one can gradually adjust the color temperature from warm white to cool white (from 2,700 K to 6,500 K), but instead they used multiple individual lamps with different fixed color temperatures. Each lamp fixture contained five LEDs whose light was blended together, allowing lighting calibration between warm white (3,000 K) and cool white (6,000 K). According to the manufacturer (Osram), the Color Rendering Index is over 95 R_a. In total, some 170,000 light-emitting diodes were installed in four different types of light fixtures: cove lighting; illuminated ceiling lighting; spotlights; and shed-roof lighting. A total of 91 preset lighting scenarios can be called up using portable tablet PCs, purportedly allowing the choice of 100 different shades of color for each artwork.

This lighting concept conforms to my approach of immersing art in the light of our zeitgeist. Even though the deployment in this particular case seems quite complex, some seven years later we already have at our disposal a selection of lighting technologies that yield similar effects. Indeed, the design tools are at hand, so now the only remaining question is how and in what form they should be implemented in an art museum.

Since the 1990s, the demands on museum architecture have increased significantly. No doubt, Frank O. Gehry's Guggenheim Museum in Bilbao (completed in 1997) raised the bar (cf. Mack 1999: 23ff.). Its spectacular architectural design became a major cultural magnet and Bilbao experienced an economic boom that positively impacted the city's development. Indeed, the term "Bilbao effect" has been coined to demonstrate how targeted cultural innovation, particularly in museum architecture, can jumpstart urban renewal. This represents a turning point in the history of cultural buildings, whose architecture has taken on a new significance among municipal officials, urban developers and builders.

As a result, many noteworthy art museums have been built around the world in recent decades, including: the Louvre in Abu Dhabi by Jean Nouvel, MOCAPE in Shenzhen by Coop Himmelb(l)au, The Broad in Los Angeles by Diller Scofidio + Renfro, Tate Modern in London by Herzog & de Meuron and MAXXI in Rome by Zaha Hadid. And our conception of the function of contemporary museum architecture has likewise changed: Nowadays, museums must not only be didactic institutions, but centers of leisure and entertainment, as well. The character profile of a museum has thus changed fundamentally over the last decades. Outstanding architecture frames art in a new, unprecedented way and a visit to an art museum becomes an unparalleled experience.

SPECIFICATIONS FOR LIGHTING IN ART MUSEUMS

The handling of artificial light in a museum seems pragmatic. This can be explained by the fact that the available illuminants in recent decades did not offer much design freedom. This can change with the deployment of dynamic lighting technology.

The planning of the lighting of a museum has to follow applicable legal standards. *EN 12464-1 Light and lighting—Lighting of work places—Part 1: Indoor work places* (edition 2021-12-15) contains the following provisions for museum lighting:

TRADE FAIRS AND EXHIBITION HALLS

Ref. no.	Type of room, task, or activity	$\bar{E}_m$		R_{UGL}	U_o	R_a	Notes
		Required[a]	Modified[b]				
39.1	General lighting	300	500	22	0,40	80	

[a] Requirement: minimum value
[b] Modified: considers common context modification in 5.3.3

△ Table 1. Photometric requirements for trade fairs according to ÖNORM EN 12464-1: 2021-12-15 Table 39

MUSEUMS

Ref. no.	Type of room, task, or activity	$\bar{E}_m$		R_{UGL}	U_o	R_a	Notes
		Required[a]	Modified[b]				
40.1	Exhibits, insensitive to light	–		–	–	80	The illumination is primarily being determined by the requirements of the exhibit.
40.2	Exhibits, sensitive to light	–		–	–	80	The illumination is primarily being determined by the requirements of the exhibit. Protection against damage is of the utmost importance. Conservation issues with respect to potential damage to the exhibit must be taken into consideration when selecting the light sources.

[a] Requirement: minimum value
[b] Modified: considers common context modification in 5.3.3

△ Table 2. Photometric requirements for museums according to ÖNORM EN 12464-1: 2021-12-15 Table 40

Though they delineate certain requirements for exhibition lighting, these specifications are not very significant. The International Council of Museums (ICOM) defines international standards for museums. In its documentation, there is only one statement related to lighting: "Exhibition architecture ensures a microclimate appropriate for the respective objects. Careful selection of harmless materials, paints and lighting is warranted, as is regular monitoring of all climate factors relevant to the inventory." (ICOM, *Standards für Museen*, 2006: 16).

It would seem that the current guidelines grant a lot of leeway when it comes to planning lighting design. As a result, lighting companies and designers are developing their own guides on the subject. The architect and lighting expert Thomas Schielke, for example, identifies six different types of exhibitions to which he assigns certain lighting characteristics. He classifies lighting for the White Cube as follows:

CHARACTERISTIC PROPERTIES FOR THE WHITE CUBE BY SCHIELKE

BRIGHTNESS CONTRAST	low
SPECTRUM	Color temperature: uniform Color rendition: high
DAYLIGHT	diffuse
LUMINAIRES	wall washer
WALL	white

△ Table 3. Schielke, *LEUKOS*, 2020, vol. 16, no. 1: 11

However, the basis of this categorization is not transparently referenced in this quoted publication. It is not clear to me whether Schielke is referring to existing White Cubes, if his opinion is intended as an ideal, or if it is simply a guideline for planning. Assuming that this table is meant to be a planning aid and that one conceives a White Cube based on Schielke's description, the result would be a room with white walls and an illuminated ceiling that diffuses daylight. The walls are artificially illuminated by wall washers. Such White Cubes are uncommon. Typically, the ceiling is opaque so that no overhead natural light enters the space. The illuminants vary according to the different generations and developments of lighting technologies—these days, wall washers are seldom used. The characteristics described here are inconsistent with the White Cubes I have surveyed. My own measurements show that the color temperatures often vary, the Color Rendering Index is usually rather low, and the spaces are outfitted with ceiling spots, track spots, or fluorescent lamps rather than with wall washers.

In my opinion, this table is not a potential guideline for the White Cubes of the future, as it does not provide us designers the necessary flexibility enabling us to satisfy the demands of contemporary art presentation. I am not talking about a hyperrealistic display in the sense of Schielke (2020), but rather creating a dynamic-light display in dialogue with artists and curators. In this context, light is viewed as a versatile protagonist and intermediary between art and the viewer. The point is to recognize the potential of dynamic-lighting technologies and deploy them flexibly. However, this requires that we plan for these technologies when designing a White Cube, equipping it with intelligent lighting systems that create a White Space that nevertheless embodies all facets of natural light. For it is the White Cube's lighting that shapes the atmosphere and our perception, allowing us to experience art emotionally.

Ever since the White Cube has existed as an exhibition space, the light quality of the artificial illuminants has not been called into question, although it is a key parameter that determines the visual perception of the art displayed in the exhibition space and shapes its atmosphere. The White Cube is meant to be a white, neutral space in which nothing should distract the viewer's attention from the art. But if the focus is shifted to the lighting and one examines various light configurations within diverse White Cubes, they are not nearly as neutral or as neutralizing as previously thought.

The results of light surveys at several Viennese galleries and museums show that lighting in the respective exhibition spaces varies greatly in all aspects, especially when it comes to color temperature. The spectra of their respective illuminants—the DNA of light—also reveals significant differences among the spaces. In one gallery, we experience art under a full spectrum of warm white light, while another space is suffused with only a narrow spectrum of cold white light. What effect does this have on the atmosphere and our perception of the space? Do these aspects determine how we perceive art? What impact does lighting make on a space's architecture?

As an architect, I have often been involved in the design and planning process of a museum (cf. Mönninger 2010). The first step for an architect faced with the task of designing a museum is to address its spatial and functional program. This includes the proportions of spaces, their layouts relative to each other and, above all, the characteristics given to each space. For a concert hall, the focus is primarily on its acoustics, which along with the lighting and materials shape the atmosphere, character and quality of the building. When one considers an art museum, one would think that its principle conceptual element would be its lighting. This is basically true, but its functional requirements are not nearly as clearly defined as acoustics are for a concert hall. Everyone knows that a concert house should provide a perfect aural environment. We hear and feel music. But what about visual art? Do museums provide a perfect visual environment? How do we see and experience art?

No significant empirical guidelines for lighting can be found in connection with museum space allocation and function plans nor descriptions. One would never begin to design a concert hall without consulting an acoustician. Lighting designers for museums are usually consulted during later stages of planning. The importance is far from being equal to that of acousticians in the planning of a concert hall. A concert hall will utterly fail if the proportions and surfaces do not support the acoustic requirements. To be sure, lighting design allows for greater flexibility. This could be due to the ability of our eyes to adapt disproportionately quickly to different light conditions (cf. Fairchild et al. 1995). Artificial lighting is usually considered only when the time comes to design and furnish the interior. Conceptually, the architecture is furnished with light.

The White Cube remains a conventional exhibition space for contemporary art and should frame the art with its neutral atmosphere. A neutral space is not a dead space. An empty white room comes alive when illuminated. The White Cube of the 1980s utilized that decade's artificial lighting—much of the art was displayed under fluorescent lamps. The White Cube of the current decade is illuminated by LEDs, but one should not only consider this with regard to luminaires, but in terms of lighting—dynamic lighting.

Once we manage to comprehend artificial light as a material and design with it, it could mark the beginning of a paradigm shift in architecture, comparable to how daylight was seen as an essential design parameter during the Gothic era.

STATUS OF RESEARCH

To determine what is the best lighting for art in museums, several research studies have examined how art is perceived under different lighting conditions. The focus is usually on Correlated Color Temperature (CCT), Color Rendering Index (CRI) and illuminance (*E*). Previous studies' results are astonishingly different and provide us with few answers regarding what the best lighting should be for displaying contemporary art. When it comes to color temperature, for example, studies have issued contradictory findings. While Scuello, Abramov, Gorden, and Weintraub (cf. Scuello et al. 2003) determined that the ideal color temperature for illuminating artworks is 3,600 Kelvin, Pridmore's study (cf. Pridmore 2017) suggests that a color temperature between 4,500 K and 5,500 K is preferable.

In today's art museums, one usually finds lamps emitting a color temperature of around 3,000 K. This could be for conservation purposes, as the potential for damage to artworks is reduced at lower color temperatures, due to their shorter wavelengths. However, it could be explained by the simple fact that, in recent decades, most museums have used halogen spotlights, which typically have a color temperature of between 2,700 K and 3,200 K. The choice of light temperature around 3,000 K in the museum is also often justified by Kruithof's comfort curve. In 1941, the Dutch physicist Arie Andries Kruithof discovered a relationship between color temperature and illuminance (lux) when it comes to our perception of light. He determined that we find pleasing low color temperatures with low illuminance (e.g. 2,200–2,500 K at 50 lux) and higher color temperatures with higher illuminance (e.g. 2,700–3,600 K at 200 lux). Among experts, his findings are controversial and have been refuted over and over (cf. Davis et al. 1990).

While museum experts (conservators, curators, directors, exhibition and lighting designers) base their choice of optimal lighting mainly for purposes of art conservation, the viewing public set their preference according to visual criteria—primarily on lighting's impact (visibility, color rendering and attractiveness) upon the pictures (cf. Kesner 1993). Interestingly enough, few records currently exist about how museum professionals choose lighting. Garside et al. (2017) sought to fill this knowledge gap by conducting interviews with twelve museum professionals in Great Britain. Although there are numerous guidelines and codes of practice on the subject of museum lighting, a wide range of processes for selecting lighting was observed.

It seems there is no uniform set of rules that dictates the choice of museum lighting. Garside also found that museum professionals value visual testing highly—through trial and error, they adjust the lighting on site accordingly.

In contrast to experts, how does the visiting public prefer lighting, when they are given a choice? As already mentioned in detail, previous studies have shown that viewers' preferences for color temperature of the lighting are quite different. While conducting our own Case Study 01, we also had the opportunity to get to the bottom of this matter, as we allowed the test viewer to choose the color temperature freely. The results varied considerably. The lowest value was 2,919 K and the highest was 5,328 K (cf. Pelowski, Leder, Graser et al. 2019: 6). This wide range of results reinforced our assumption that the perception of light is very subjective. This could also explain why the results of previous studies diverge so broadly.

For example, Scuello et al. (2004) found a preference for a color temperature of 3,600 K (halogen lamps), when viewers were given a range of options between 2,500 K and 7,000 K, at illuminance levels between 200 and 250 lux. Postcard reproductions of paintings were mounted in matte black frames and hung, one at the time, on the rear wall of each room. Nascimento and Masuda (2014), on the other hand, reached a very different conclusion, finding that 5,700 K was the preferred color temperature. The subjects of this study viewed artworks displayed on a video screen and could choose from a range of lighting levels between 3,600 K and 20,000 K provided by an adjustable (Tunable White) illuminant. They arrived at a similar conclusion when conducting the research using real artworks within a gallery setting. Their illumination had a much higher CCT value compared to that used in previous studies, which could explain the different result. However, a study by Pino, Lanhars and Nascimento (2006, 2008) used illuminants in the range of 2,856 K and 6,000 K and nevertheless arrived at a comparable result—a preferred color temperature of 5,100 K (330 lux). The 11 artworks selected for this study were also digitally displayed on screen.

The study by Feltrin and others (2017) took a similar approach to our second experiment, *Five Artists × Five Museums*. In Feltrin's study, an image could be viewed under five different light settings (3,000 K; 3,500 K; 4,000 K; 5,000 K and 6,000 K).

Results demonstrated that there was no clear preference among the five choices. The images were displayed against three different colored backgrounds: white, gray or black—here, too, no clear preferences were noted. For this study, reproductions of artwork (printed on canvas) were used.

With one exception, all the studies described so far have not used real artworks. But can one really determine the impact of art when one uses reproductions or even digital-screen displays of paintings? The fact that the chosen research venues were not set up to resemble an exhibition space seems equally dubious. No attention was paid to the important impact of the spatial surroundings to the artwork. Both criteria were essential factors in our own research. From the outset, it was important to me that real artwork should be shown in a real context; To this end, the art-historically tried-and-true White Cube exhibition space should be used. In consultation with curators, gallerists, artists and perception researchers, we also made a very deliberate selection of art to use in all our experiments.

To get to the bottom of the question of the ideal color temperature for a work of art, Pridmore (2017) also chose a real-world context. His research focuses on the illumination of Jackson Pollock's painting *Blue Poles* in the National Gallery of Australia. According to Pridmore, *Blue Poles* had always been displayed under warm, yellowish light, for conservation reasons. His research results called for lighting it with a color temperature of around 5,000 K, because it is under such light that the artwork truly comes alive. Pridmore's research thus draws a connection between the art on display and the colors and lighting used by the artist.

This perspective played an essential role in our selection of the picture series *Spectrum* for our research studies. For this series, the artist Friedrich Biedermann used colors that he derived from the color temperatures of light reproduced in our study's experiment spaces. He deliberately chose colors that appear more prominent under specific lighting settings, which were adopted for Case Study 01 and were preset and verified during a trial run in Research Space 02.

Portraiture, landscape and abstract oil painting were the subjects of research by Yoshizawa and others (2013). The art was displayed in a gallery mockup (white walls, wood floors). The study explored the interconnection between the painting's impasto and the color temperature (CCT), as well as between the visibility and CCT.

A study by Zhai et al. was the first in which atmosphere also played a role in the evaluation. Six oil paintings with different motifs (portrait of a man, portrait of a woman, landscape, three still lifes—all painted in an Impressionistic manner) were shown. When the test subjects rated the paintings in terms of mood and artistic background (relaxation, warm, soft, artistic), their preference was for a lower color temperature (no more than 2,850 K). When rating according to contrast, brightness, clarity and quality, viewers preferred a higher color temperature (as high as 5,000 K). This study once again demonstrates that the question about which lighting is best for art proves to be quite complicated to answer, as visual perception is influenced by many more factors than a basic choice of illuminant.

Therefore, we tried to take an antithetical approach with our experiments. The main reason for this is that our research was conducted in the context of both art and exhibition architecture. We considered the space, the art and the lighting as one system, and thus we created realistic settings.

The test subjects (in Case Studies 01, 02 and 03) were not informed that light was the subject of our studies, rather they were asked to form opinions about the art. The viewers' focus was on the artwork, as it would be in a real exhibition context.

In addition, artistic research is an integral part of the exhibition program at the AIL (Angewandte Interdisciplinary Lab), where artworks and artistic research processes are often exhibited in a gallery context. Artistic research lies at the intersection of art and science. At AIL, therefore, we were dealing with an audience that was engaged not only with the art itself, but also with issues of scientific approaches to art. They were no strangers to being actively involved in our exhibitions (Case Study 02 and 03). This resulted in a very natural and realistic approach to art. The empirical data generated by our case studies are authentic and do not come from an unnatural laboratory environment. The audience actively participates in our experiments.

Furthermore, our goal was not to determine the perfect lighting for any particular artwork, but rather the focus was on how our visual perception of art can be enhanced by dynamic lighting. If we bear in mind that one's visual perception is influenced by one's past and present viewing experiences, one could argue that we have succeeded in enhancing the audience's experience and challenging our viewing habits.

Since previous studies addressing the question of the best lighting for art have yielded such varied results, and the perception of light (as well as art) is obviously very subjective, the question of the potential of artificial light sources should be approached without reservation. I find it entirely reasonable to deploy dynamic lighting *dynamically*, to support the sensory experience of art, and to link the audience to the art through the lighting. Why shouldn't we mimic a natural resource like daylight to bolster art's ability to communicate? Considering that we experience our world in three dimensions through light and in color, we should use dynamic light in architecture to restore all tangible and sensual qualities to artificially illuminated spaces and objects, so that we may experience them with all our senses.

THE POTENTIAL FOR DYNAMIC LIGHTING IN MUSEUMS

If we conceive of artificial lighting in an exhibition space as merely static illumination, then we perceive that space and the art on display only under that particular lighting. For example, if a gallery's artificial light comes from fluorescent tubes, one experiences the space exclusively under this light. The fluorescent tube usually has a color temperature of 4,000 K and emits only a fraction of the colors of the spectrum. In addition, the Color Rendering Index of most fluorescent tubes is well below 80 R_a. Ever since artificial lighting was invented, the perception of artificially illuminated spaces has been limited to specific static color temperatures, their spectra and color-rendering qualities. Has this categorically inhibited our perception of exhibition spaces and art? How might lighting technologies with dynamically variable color temperatures, full spectra, high color-rendering values and variable light intensities affect our perception of art and exhibition spaces? Moreover, there is a nonvisual aspect to the perception of light, which was demonstrated in 2002 (Berson et al. 2002). Dynamic artificial lighting, like natural daylight, can impact our sense of well-being.

PERCEPTION OF DYNAMIC LIGHTING

We differentiate between the *visual* and *nonvisual* perception of light. The latter is of great importance in connection with dynamic artificial lighting, with which the melanopic effect of light is brought into play by means of targeted adjustments to color temperature and intensity. Whether or not we perceive it visually, light must first pass through the eye before it becomes processed in different ways.

VISUAL PERCEPTION

The human eye is sensitive to light with wavelengths between approximately 380 and 750 nanometers—the range we humans can experience directly. The human eye has adapted to this range because these wavelengths enable maximal visibility in sunlight. Although the sun emits other wavelengths, the Earth's atmosphere filters out all but those in this range, to which our eyes and brain have adapted (cf. Bachmann 2006, essay by Fischer: 98). It is relatively easy for us to distinguish between cold white light and warm white light. We describe the difference in terms of different colors of white light. However, we cannot *see* light itself—light must always strike an object in order for us to perceive and describe it in such terms. Even common dust particles allow us to sense light; how a car's headlight beam becomes visible to us as a cone of light, for example.

The human eye enables vision by means of its visual perception of light. The eye absorbs light rays via the retina (cones and rods) and transmits them to the brain. While the cones permit us to perceive colors, the more light-sensitive rods allow us to see in twilight. The human eye can adjust surprisingly quickly to different lighting conditions. For example, it has been demonstrated that the eye can adapt to 90 percent of new lighting conditions within 60 seconds (cf. Fairchild et al. 1995).

Although this adjustment occurs quite quickly, it has been empirically shown that significantly less time is spent in front of an artwork in an exhibition. According to the lighting expert, Prof. Tran Quoc Khanh (who has been head of the Laboratory of Lighting Technology at the Technical University of Darmstadt for many years), the luminaire's effect on humans is based on three components: brightness, color quality and nonvisual perception.

NONVISUAL PERCEPTION

In 2002, it was demonstrated that light is sensed not only by the eye, but also by the pineal gland (epiphysis), through which the melanopic effect of light is perceived (cf. Berson et al. 2002). Descartes already suspected that some connection existed between the eyes and the pineal gland, which is located at the back of the midbrain. He saw the pineal gland as the central interpreter of vision (cf. Becker 2009: 57). The pineal gland releases the hormone melatonin, which regulates our biological clock and sleep-wake rhythms. Melatonin secretion is increased at night. The pineal gland—the so-called "third eye"—and its release of melatonin play an increasingly important role in the development of artificial daylight—Human Centric Lighting. The day-night rhythm is a circadian rhythm, a pattern that repeats itself every 24 hours.

Clearly, the notion of this "third eye" also influences our perception of space and architecture. Research is currently taking place worldwide on the topic of melatonin and artificial light (e.g., Hurlbert et al. 2016) and it is becoming apparent that artificial light sources impact how we feel and influence our sleep rhythms. Various scientific studies show how lighting systems that simulate the natural course of daylight in schools, offices and shops have a lasting impact on people's health and well-being. For example, in 2016 the Oktalite company conducted research in two supermarkets over a ten-month period. It found that that use of HCL (Human Centric Lighting) lengthened the duration of shoppers' visits and increased their purchases. Another study (cf. Wiggerich 2017), demonstrated that HCL impacts the well-being of employees, whose sick days decreased significantly.

The existing studies on museum lighting have been limited to its impact on visual perception, but no comparable study on the non-visual perception of museum lighting can be found. Considering how museumgoers approach art intuitively, attention should be paid to the impact of artificial light sources upon our emotions in the museum context. Dynamic artificial lighting could be used to facilitate viewers' perception of art on an emotional level. But what is dynamic artificial light, how is it manufactured and what quality criteria should it meet?

DYNAMIC ARTIFICIAL LIGHTING WITH INTELLIGENT CONTROL SYSTEMS

In the context of lighting, "dynamic" describes lighting that varies over a given period of time as a result of regulating one or more of its parameters—for example, its intensity, luminous color or direction.

While special dynamic lighting technologies can render all colors in the RGB spectrum, my investigations focused exclusively on light sources that can simulate dynamic white light and daylight. This is what the lighting industry likes to refer to as Human Centric Lighting (HCL), a term that does not describe a specific lighting technology but rather light sources whose color temperatures and intensity can be dynamically adjusted to emulate sequences of daylight.

Deployment of dynamic light sources requires the use of an intelligent lighting-control system such as Casambi (Bluetooth). Two different control systems were used in our experiment setup: DMX and ZigBee. DMX (Digital MultipleX) is a wired system using the Loxone Smart-Home software to program the lighting, while ZigBee is operated via a wireless network and uses myPi-LED software provided by the manufacturer. Both systems allowed us to preset the light sources numerically (color temperature / XY coordinates) and via controllers (lux) and to activate them according to light values recorded at mumok (Vienna's Museum of Modern and Contemporary Art). The myPi-LED software allowed us to program and reproduce different dynamic sequences, as well.

So, when we talk about dynamic light sources, it means that their intensity and color temperature can be changed. If the course of the sun (3,200 K at dawn to 5,500 K at high noon) is depicted in the color triangle, it lies exactly on Planck's curve (see fig. 9, below).

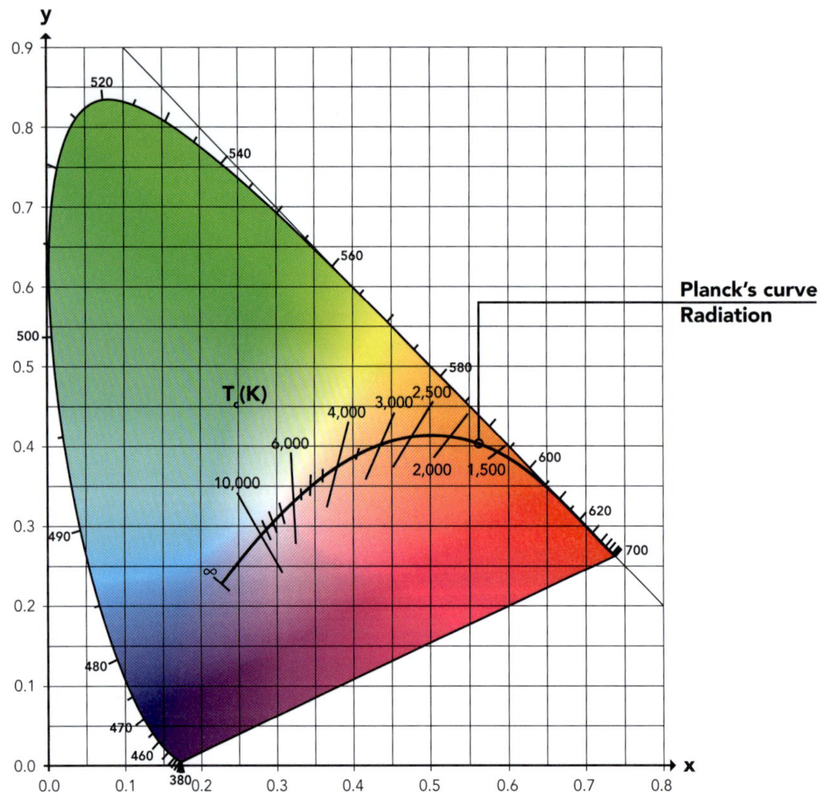

△ Figure 9. CIE 1931 xy Color triangle with Planck's curve/ Radiation (Black-body Locus)

The illuminant PiLED used for our experiment setup is capable of simulating dynamic white light that exactly follows Planck's curve, unlike the x-y values of many common light sources that emit white light. Take, for example, the lighting measured in Vienna's subway cars. Here, the values of the illuminants lie above Plank's curve on the x-y axes (see fig. 10, below). If the deviation is too large, the light no longer appears to be pure white.

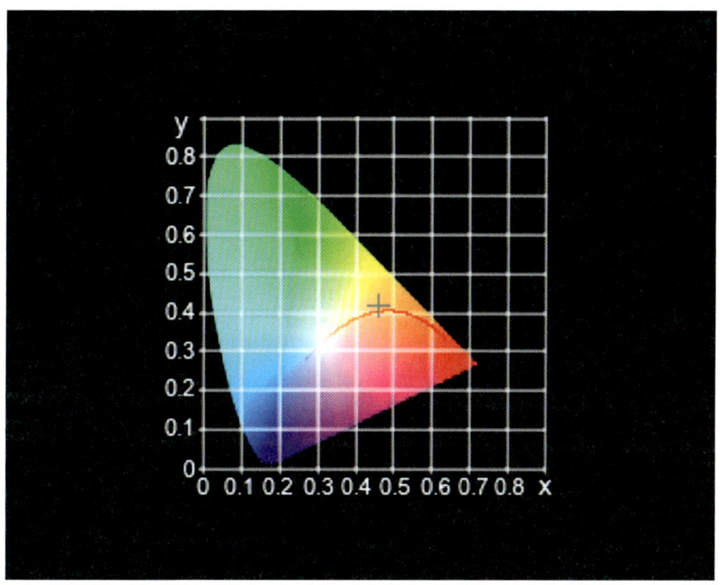

△ Figure 10. Color triangle light measurement with digital spectrometer, Vienna subway, 13 October 2019

QUALITY CHARACTERISTICS OF WHITE LIGHT

As designers, we bring the sun into the space in the form of dynamic artificial lighting and can deploy it flexibly. But what are the properties of white light and how can these properties be used in design?

COLOR TEMPERATURE

The color shades of visible white light (along Planck's curve) can be ascribed to various color temperatures [Kelvin (K)]. We describe light in this context as cold or warm. The following classification can be found in the European standard (EN 12464-1:2021):

CLASSIFICATION OF COLOR TEMPERATURES

LIGHT COLOR	CORRELATED COLOR TEMPERATURE (in K)
Warm white	≤ 3,300
Cool white	3,300–5,300
Daylight white	≥ 5,300

△ Table 4. Light color and closest color temperature of lamps according to EN 12464-1

For example, the spectrometer gives me readings in the range of 1,500 K to 2,100 K for candlelight, depending on the particular candle tested. These values lie on the far right of Planck's curve in the color triangle. The Kelvin values of daylight range from ~2,000 K to ~20,000 K, depending on the time of day and cloud cover and whether one is measuring direct sunlight or diffuse sky radiation. There are no standards for how to plan the application of light color. Over the past decades, designers deploying artificial lighting have been dependent on light sources that (compared with daylight) only render a specific static color temperature within a range (see table 5).

COLOR TEMPERTURES OF LIGHT SOURCES

LIGHT SOURCE	**COLOR TEMPERATURE** (sample values in K)
Candlelight	1,500–2,100
Incandescent lamp	2,600–3,000
Halogen lamp	2,700–3,400
Fluorescent lamp	~ 4,000
Dawn/dusk	2,000–3,400
Midday sun	5,500–5,800
Blue hour (skylight when the sun sinks below horizon)	9,000–12,000 K
Skylight (clear blue northern skylight)	15,000–27,000

△ Table 5. Overview of color temperatures of common artificial light sources compared to natural light

This is now different with LEDs. We now have at our disposal a wide range of color temperatures by deploying both fixed white LEDs and color-changeable LEDs. It is now possible with LEDs to bathe art in the color temperature of, for example, candlelight or daylight.

SPECTRUM

Color temperature describes only the luminous color of an illuminant but does not provide any information about the mixture ratio of the spectral colors. Two illuminants can have identical color temperatures, although their spectra differ significantly. If you analyze the spectrum for each respective illuminant, striking differences in quality become apparent. Compared to sunlight, which is characterized by its full spectrum, fluorescent lighting, for example, has an incomplete spectrum; some color components are missing. This can be seen clearly when looking through a handheld spectroscope (see fig. 11).

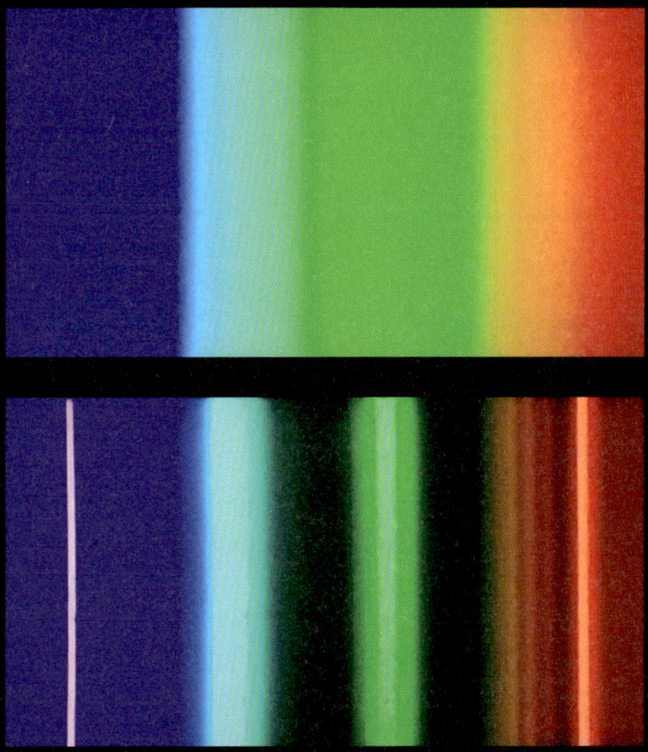

△ Figure 11. Photographed through a spectroscope (on 11 March 2020): *top*, continuous spectrum of sunlight; *bottom*, discontinuous line spectrum of an 11 W (equivalent) compact fluorescent lamp

To this day, fluorescent tubes are still used in many exhibition spaces. They are commonly used in skylight areas (e.g., Kunsthaus Bregenz, Museum of Applied Arts Vienna, Kunsthistorisches Museum Vienna). In recent decades, most skylights have completely blocked out natural light and are instead artificially backlit. Due to its high potential for damage, daylight was shunned and replaced by mediocre light sources, contrary to the original architectural conceptions for these spaces. The image produced by the handheld spectrometer when held up to fluorescent lighting makes it plain to see that some colors of the spectrum are missing, replaced by black bars (see fig. 11). It should go without saying that such incomplete light affects our perception of art.

The color impression of an illuminated object depends on the spectral composition of the light and a natural color impression is only possible if the entire spectrum is present. Daylight has a Color Rendering Index (CRI) of 100 R_a, the highest value on this scale. Illuminants with high R_a values lend the illuminated object a natural appearance. The lower this value is, the less intense the colors of an illuminated object appear. A high R_a is essential for an art museum, but not a given. Up to now, according to ÖNORM EN 12464-1, a value of 80 R_a has been acceptable. The potential of a light source to cause damage depends on its spectrum. As the 380–400 nanometer (nm) range represents the most high-energy and thus most harmful part of visible radiation, it also makes sense in museums to filter out visible light < 400 nm, as well as UV light. This is the case with most LEDs, which also produce no harmful UV and IR radiation and thus pose no threat of damaging artwork. In deploying dynamic artificial light systems, intelligent controls could further minimize the duration of harmful light exposure.

COLOR RENDERING

Color rendering values are expressed by using the CRI (Color Rendering Index—R_a) scale, which compares the quality of an artificial light source to natural light. CRI 1931, the Color Rendering Index introduced in 1931, used eight test colors. Only pastels were selected, because of the high red-light content of the commercially available lamps at that time. As early as the 1960s, with the advent of the fluorescent lamp, saturated colors were added as standards by the International Commission on Illumination (CIE) and enshrined in *CIE Publication 13.3*. Due to the rapid development of LED lighting technologies, with which spectral composition can vary greatly, there is an ongoing need for revising the standards. The most recent publication, *CIE 13.03-2015*, prescribes 14 test colors as reference values, which are listed in the *DIN 6169*. The selection of test colors is the subject of ongoing debate among professionals, as well as in connection with exhibition lighting. For example, in their article *Museumsbeleuchtung Teil 1* (Museum Lighting Part 1) in the trade journal *LICHT* (1-2/2013), Pepler and his team from the Technical University of Darmstadt allege that the 14 CIE colors do not exhibit the spectral bandwidth typical of oil paints or watercolors.

The CRI value of a luminaire indicates the visible quality of the test colors illuminated by it. The CRI scale goes from 0 to 100. The higher the value, the more natural the illuminated objects appear. The CRI, like color-temperature values, does not provide any information about the exact spectral composition and weighting of the individual spectral colors. As shown in figure 12 on page 83, the CRI values of 90 and 91 are nearly identical, but there are striking differences in the spectral images.

Nevertheless, the Color Rendering Index is an essential quality factor when illuminating a work of art, and the qualitative differences between a lamp with CRI 80 and one with CRI 90 are visible to the naked eye.

ILLUMINANCE

Even at an illuminance of one lux, a digital spectrometer yields precise measurements of spectrum, color rendering value and color temperature of light (see fig. 13). Accordingly, illuminance has no impact on the quality of light—its DNA. Therefore, this factor does not play an important role in our experiments on the perception of light, even though illuminance has often been correlated (incorrectly) with color temperature ever since Kruithof.

Museums generally prescribe values between 50 and 200 lux for conservation reasons. It should be noted, however, that this standard did not stem from any art-conservation study, but from *The Museum Environment* (Thomson 1986: 25ff.), a study dealing with visual preferences. It seems that such benchmarks for maximum illuminance of light-sensitive artwork has nevertheless crept into museum guidelines.

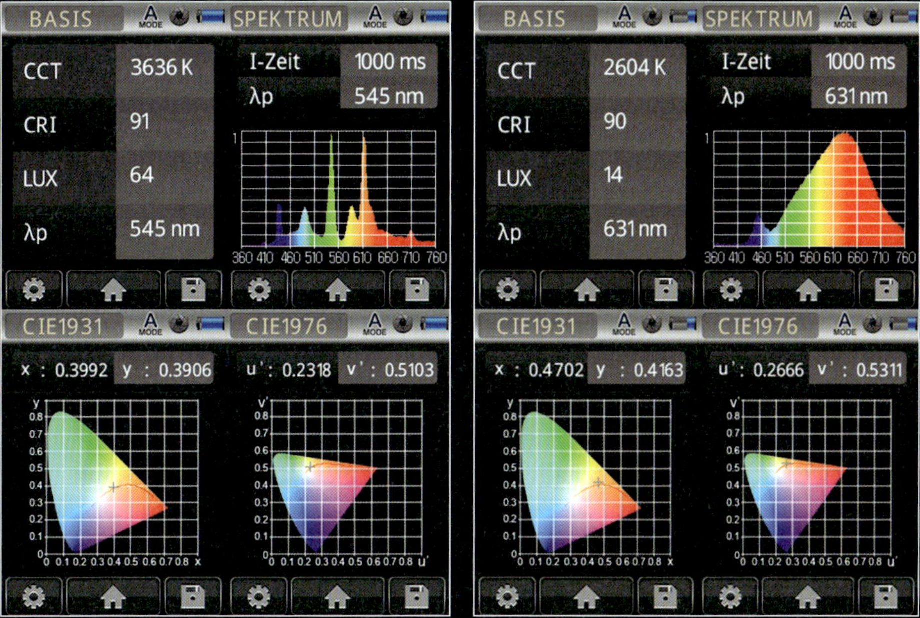

△ Figure 12. Measurement results: comparison of spectrum at CRI 90 and CRI 91

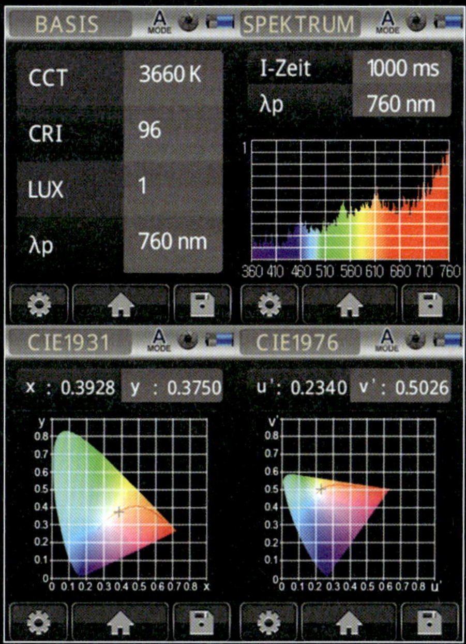

MANUFACTURING PROCESS OF ARTIFICIAL WHITE LED LIGHT

With regard to sunlight, white light consists of a blend of different spectral colors. The technical term for this is *polychromatic* light. If one assumes light is a wave phenomenon, polychromatic light is a composite of many wavelengths. If light is considered to be particulate (corpuscular), polychromatic light consists of photons of various energies. Monochromatic light, on the other hand, has only one wavelength or a single photon power, and is visible as a single color.

The light-emitting diode (LED) is a semiconductor device consisting of inorganic materials, with the properties of a diode that emits light under the influence of electrical voltage. When an electric current flows in the forward direction, it emits light depending on the semiconductor material used and its doping. While conventional incandescent lamps always emit a continuous spectrum of light, an LED can be used to emit light of a very specific color. It is essentially dependent on the semiconductor material used.

(translated from Ris 2019: 141)

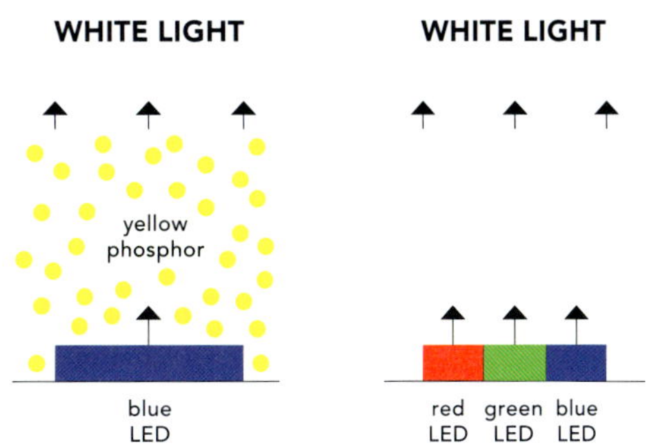

△ Figure 14. Schematic diagrams of pc-LED *(left)* and RGB LED *(right)*

TWO COMMON METHODS FOR PRODUCING WHITE LEDS

There are two common methods for creating an LED that emits white light: the phosphor-converted method and the RGB method (see fig. 14).

With the phosphor method, a thin phosphor layer is applied over a blue LED. It yields monochromatic light, which means that unlike sunlight, this white light is generated as a single wavelength. The RGB method, on the other hand, produces polychromatic light—its white light is created by blending the colors red, green and blue.

Polychromatic light can be demonstrated with a simple experiment. If one takes three spotlights (red, green, blue) and overlaps their beams, one gets white light. The person in figure 15 blocks the slightly offset spotlights and therefore the fundamental colors become evident in the lights' projection.

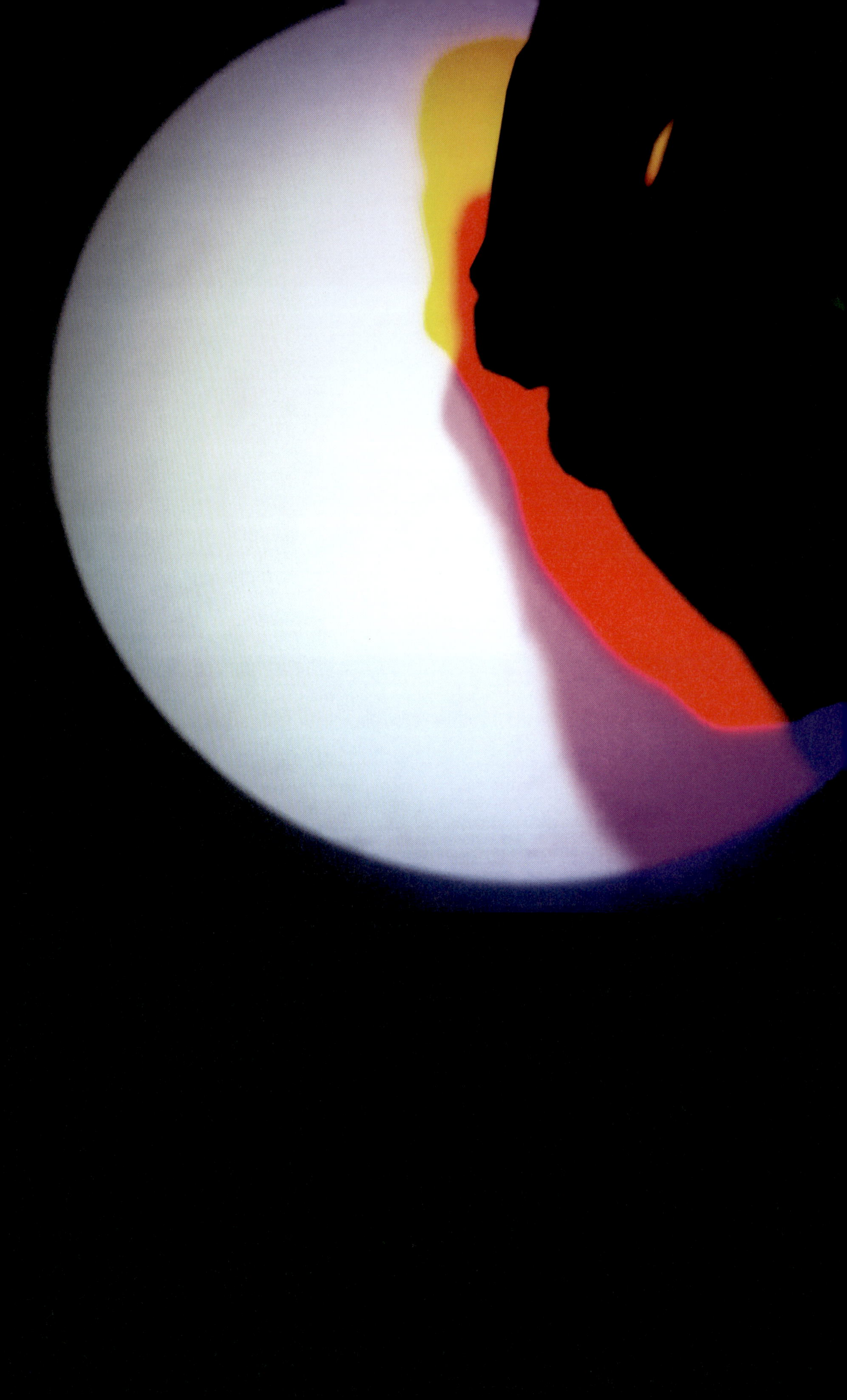

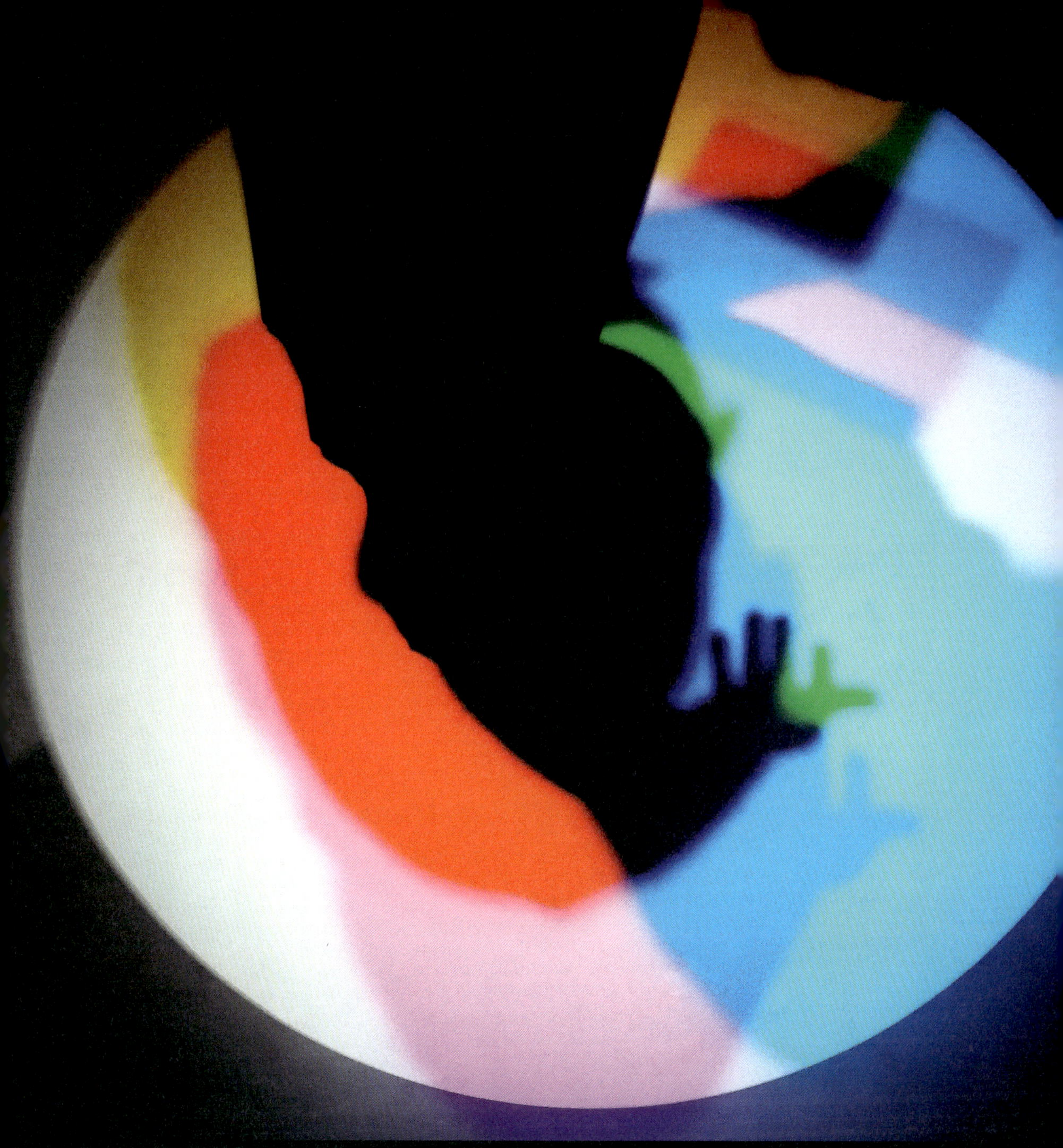

△ Figure 15. Photos: experiment, 18 February 2020, three colored spots with overlapping beams

PRODUCTION OF DYNAMIC WHITE LIGHT BY TWO- AND THREE-CHANNEL SYSTEMS

Two-channel (warm white and cool white) or three-channel (RGB) systems are typically used to produce dynamic white light. There are systems with five or more channels, as well.

The two-channel system is known as "Tunable White." It enables dynamic white-light gradients ranging from 2,500 K to 6,500 K. Because the Tunable White system consists of two channels, it is only possible to generate a gradient between the different color temperatures. If one tries to reproduce a range larger than 2,500 K to 6,500 K with this method, its middle range deviates from Planck's curve too much, which directly impacts the quality of white light.

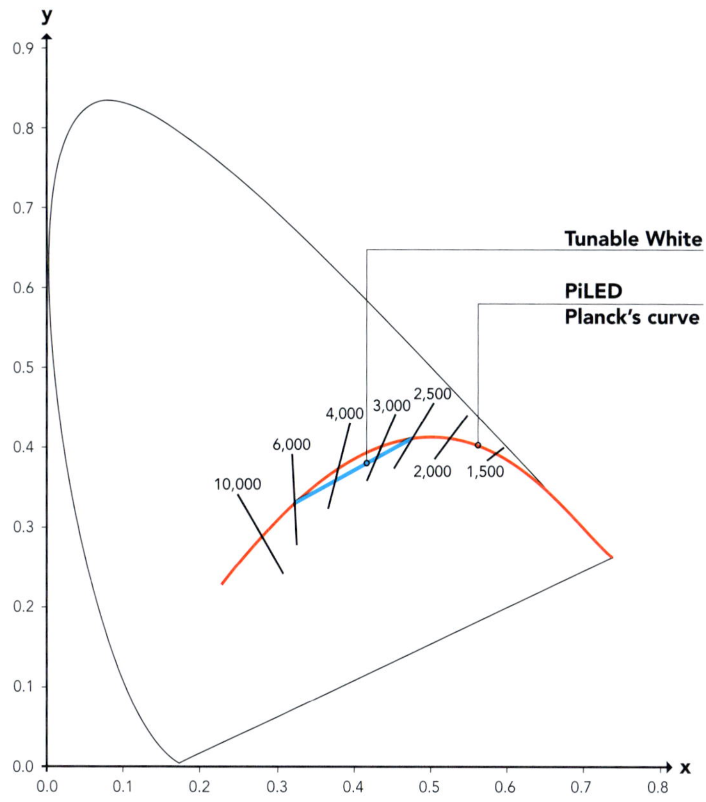

△ Figure 16. Graph: gradient of dynamic white light (Tunable White) compared with PiLED

Since 2014, I have been interested in a lighting technology patented in 2008. It emerged as a visionary technology in 2018, due to its control system. Companies such as Osram and Philips have entered into licensing agreements to build such controls into their Tunable White systems. Unlike commercially available RGB systems, the three-channel PiLED replaces the green light-emitting diode with a mint-colored one, augmenting the standard red and blue LEDs. This makes it possible to generate comparatively higher-quality white light. This method of color mixing, developed by the physicist Hans Hoschopf, enables a continuously variable rendering of white light exactly along Planck's curve, thus yielding considerably more color temperatures that can be rendered with Tunable White (see fig. 16, above). The PiLED can dynamically render all color temperatures in the range from 1,800 K to 16,000 K (CRI > 90) along the curve.

LIGHT MEASUREMENT

The quality attributes of light described previously in this chapter can be measured and imaged using a digital spectrometer. A spectrometer for measuring light can analyze the component colors of light radiation, its individual wavelengths. Spectral measurement originated in 1800 with Friedrich Wilhelm Herschel, who observed that the filters used in his telescope heated up differently depending on their color. This led him to explore the thermal effects of the solar spectrum and his findings formed the basis of spectral analysis.

In 1814, Joseph Fraunhofer developed an apparatus with which he discovered that the solar spectrum contains quite a few dark lines (see also fig. 11), known today as "Fraunhofer lines" (cf. Heilmann 2013: 20ff.).

A UPRtek MK350 series portable digital spectrometer was used to measure the lighting within existing exhibition spaces, as well as to verify the light settings of our experiment setups. This device analyzes and images the Correlated Color Temperature (CCT), Color Rendering Index (CRI), Illuminance (E), peak wavelength (λp), CIE color space including color coordinates, as well as the spectrum. The data were stored digitally.

MEASUREMENT OF ESTABLISHED MUSEUMS

Surveys of lighting in established galleries and art museums formed the basis of the White Cube Teleporter research project.

MEASUREMENT METHOD

A portable spectrometer (UPRtek Series MK350) was used for measurements. This device analyzes and displays the spectrum (see fig. 17), as well as the Correlated Color Temperature (CCT), the Color Rendering Index (CRI), the Illuminance (*E*), the peak wavelength (λp) and the CIE color space including color coordinates.

Before beginning each series of measurements, the device underwent dark calibration.

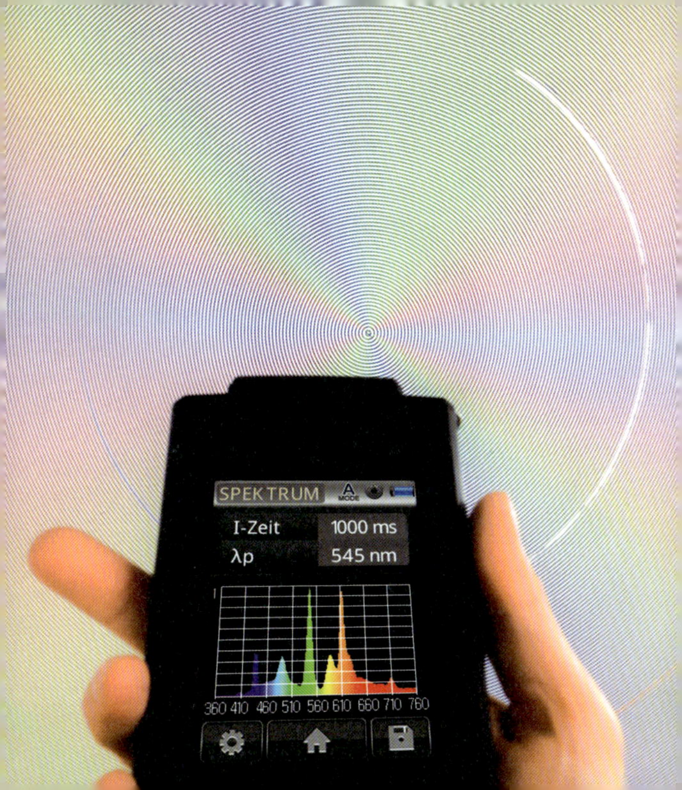

SPEKTRUM
A
MODE
I-Zeit
1000 ms
λp
545 nm
360 410 460 510 560 610 660 710 760

METERING LOCATION AND ORIENTATION

Lighting measurements were carried out in three sequential processes. These processes, as well as the alignments of the spectrometer, were developed in coordination with Prof. Günther Leising (Graz University of Technology).

FIRST MEASUREMENT

The initial measurement was conducted from the center of the room (Measurement Point 1). The device was held by hand horizontally at a height of 130 cm (~4' 3"). It was oriented so that the meter pointed from the center of the room to one of its four corners. After a first measurement was taken, the device was rotated clockwise to measure each of the remaining corners. Because the device measures spherically, this method allowed the lighting of the entire three-dimensional exhibition space to be measured.

SECOND MEASUREMENT

Another measurement was performed from Measurement Point 2, which was located at a distance of 120 cm (~3' 11") from an exhibition wall at a height of 130 cm (~4' 3"). For this measurement process, a small tube was attached to the front of the spectrometer's sensor in order to focus the measuring beam. For this measurement process, we made sure that the targeted exhibition wall was painted white and that no art was displayed on it.

THIRD MEASUREMENT

The final step was to position the device in front of an exhibited object on the wall. A reading was made when the device was pointed in the direction of the light source illuminating the object.

An example of the three measurement points and their respective orientation, based on two exhibition spaces of different sizes, is shown in figure 18.

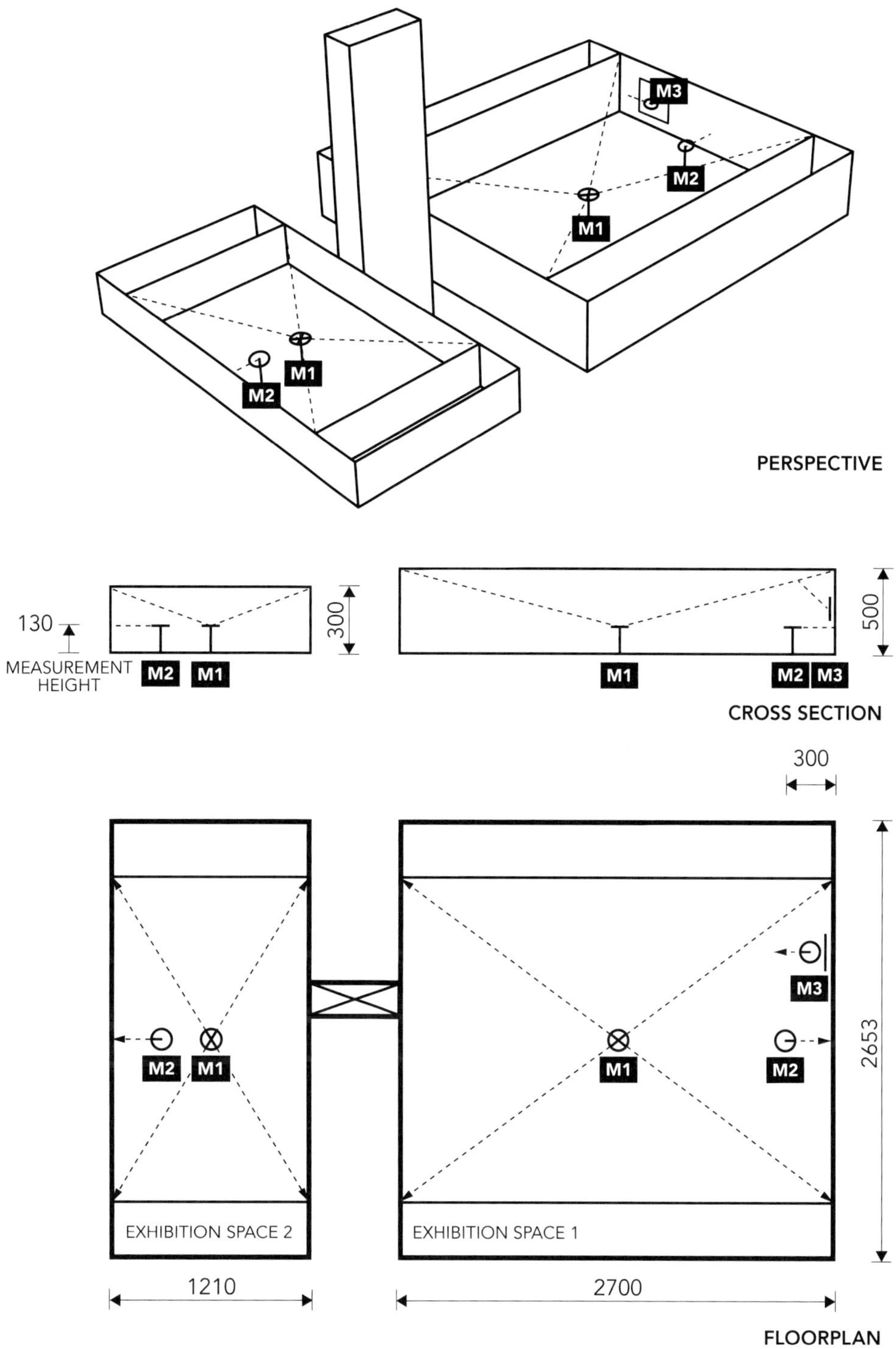

M1 Measurement Point 1: center of room / height=130 cm

M2 Measurement Point 2: 300 cm from center of wall / height=130 cm

M3 Measurement Point 3: from displayed object toward its light source

△ Figure 18. Example of measurement points and orientation in two rooms

OVERVIEW OF SURVEYED MUSEUMS

Light measurements of established galleries and art museums for the White Cube Teleporter research project were taken between June 2016 and March 2019. The research project obtained advance approvals for this purpose from the respective institutions. The results stem from state-of-the-art (at the time of the surveys) measurement devices. The values measured for each gallery space were averaged to determine the settings to be used for the subsequent research spaces. For example, all nine exhibition spaces of mumok (Vienna's Museum of Modern and Contemporary Art) were measured and compared with each other so that light settings could be benchmarked for the research project's experimental space.

The process of surveying light in museums was a continually fascinating experience throughout my research work. Over the past decades, I have seen numerous exhibitions in most of the museums, so the buildings were familiar to me. Nevertheless, I gained an entirely new perspective during the measurement process, as my attention was focused exclusively on the lighting and the space rather than on the artwork. The following table itemizes the surveyed museums, along with information on the survey date, the number and names of the surveyed rooms, the exhibitions at the time of the survey, and basic information about the museum architecture.

MUSEUM	MEASUREMENT DATE	ROOMS MEASURED	EXHIBITIONS AT TIME OF MEASUREMENT	BASIC INFO ON THE MUSEUM'S ARCHITECTURE
MUMOK, VIENNA	29 Mar 2017	All gallery areas	*Construction_Reflection* (Works from the Collection Gertraud & Dieter Bogner at mumok) 25 Nov 2016–17 Apr 2017	ARCHITECTURAL CONCEPT: O&O Baukunst ZT GmbH OPENING: 2001 LIGHTING-PLAN: Kress & Adams, Köln USEABLE AREA: 14,000 m² (150,700 sq ft) EXHIBITION AREA: 4,500 m² (48,400 sq ft) STORAGE SPACE: 1,800 m² (19,400 sq ft)
SECESSION, VIENNA	7 Apr 2017 (9:00–11:00 a.m.)	Main gallery, 2nd-floor gallery, mezzanine, gallery and anteroom for the *Beethoven Frieze*	Jean-Luc Moulène *The Secession Knot (5.1)* 6 Apr–18 June 2017 (main gallery) Anoka Faruqee *The Visible Spectrum* 6–25 June 2017 (second-floor gallery)	ARCHITECTURE: Joseph Maria Olbrich, renovated in 1985/86 by architect Adolf Krischanitz. EXHIBITION AREA: c. 1,000 m² (10,750 sq ft) CONSTRUCTED: 1898 RENOVATION: planned for Aug. 2017
MUSEUM OF APPLIED ARTS (MAK), VIENNA	30 Jun 2017	Exhibition hall and design laboratory	*VIENNA BIENNALE 2017: Robots. Work. Our Future* 21 Jun–1 Dec 2017	ARCHITECTURE: Heinrich von Ferstel CONSTRUCTED: 1868–1871 OPENING: 1871 GENERAL RENOVATIONS: 1989–1993
LENTOS, LINZ	12 Aug 2017 (10:00 a.m.–noon)	2nd-floor permanent exhibition (11 rooms) and two temporary exhibition rooms/ lower level	*Marko Lulić Futurology* 30 Jun–10 Sep 2017 (and permanent exhibition)	ARCHITECTURE: Weber & Hofer Partner AG USEABLE AREA: 8,000 m² (86,100 sq ft) LENGTH: 130 m (426'7")

MUSEUM	MEASUREMENT DATE	ROOMS MEASURED	EXHIBITIONS AT TIME OF MEASUREMENT	BASIC INFO ON THE MUSEUM'S ARCHITECTURE
MUSEUM DER MODERNE, SALZBURG	12 Aug 2017	5 galleries (Mönchsberg 2:3 Rooms/ Mönchsberg 3:2 Rooms)	William Kentridge *Thick Time. Installationen und Inszenierungen* 29 Jul–25 Nov 2017 *Resonanz von Exil* 18 Jul–28 Oct 2017	ARCHITECTURE: Friedrich Poerschke Zwink Architekten Stadtplaner Remodeling GROSS FLOOR SPACE: 6,550 m² (70,000 sq ft) PLANNING/ CONSTRUCTION: 1998–2006
KUNSTFORUM, VIENNA	9 Nov 2017	8 galleries	*Gerhard Rühm* 4 Oct 2017–28 Jan 2018	ARCHITECTURE: Gustav Peichl OPENING: 1989 EXHIBITION AREA: 1,120 m² (12,000 sq ft)
KUNSTHALLE WIEN, VIENNA	24 Nov 2017	Ground-floor and 2nd-floor galleries	*Publishing as an Artistic Toolbox: 1989–2017* 8 Nov 2017–28 Jan 2018	ARCHITECTURE: Ortner und Ortner OPENING: 2001
ARNULF RAINER MUSEUM, BADEN	14 Nov 2017	All gallery areas	*Arnulf Rainer – Die Farben des Malers* 29 Apr–17 Dez 2017	ARCHITECTURE: Lottersberger Messner Architekten (former ladies' spa) RE-OPENING: 2009
AIL, VIENNA	17 Jan 2018	All gallery areas, with focus on lower-level White Cube	None	ARCHITECTURE: propeller z (Akkalay, Tschofen, Wiederin OG) OPENING: 2010

MUSEUM	MEASUREMENT DATE	ROOMS MEASURED	EXHIBITIONS AT TIME OF MEASUREMENT	BASIC INFO ON THE MUSEUM'S ARCHITECTURE
UPPER BELVEDERE, VIENNA	7 Mar 2018 (12:00 a.m.–2:00 p.m.)	All galleries	Permanent collection consisting of works from middle ages to present	ARCHITECTURE: Johann Lucas von Hildebrandt ERECTED: 1717–1726
BELVEDERE 21. MUSEUM OF CONTEMPORARY ART, VIENNA	7 Mar 2018 (2:00–3:00 p.m.)	All galleries	*Rachel Whiteread* 7 Mar–29 Jul 2018 (main gallery) *Günter Brus – Unruhe nach dem Sturm* 2 Feb–12 Aug 2018 (second floor / Gallery)	ARCHITECTURE: Karl Schwanzer (for Austrian-Pavillon World's Fair 1958, Brussels) OPENING: 20er Haus 1962; RENOVATION: Adolf Krischanitz RE-OPENING: 2011
KUNSTHISTORISCHES MUSEUM (KHM), VIENNA	18 Jan 2018	All galleries during one visit	Permanent collection	ARCHITECTURE: Gottfried Semper Carl von Hasenauer OPENING: 1891
FERDINANDEUM, INNSBRUCK	13 Feb 2018	All galleries	None (measurements taken during renovations)	ARCHITECTURE: Anton Mutschlechner OPENING: 1845 PREVIOUS RENOVATION: 1998
LEOPOLD MUSEUM, VIENNA	9 Mar 2019	All galleries during one visit	*Wege ins Freie – von Waldmüller bis Schindler* 6 Dec 2018–28 Apr 2019 *Gustav Klimt* 6 Dec 2018–10 Mar 2019 *Egon Schiele – reloaded* 28 Sept 2018–10 Mar 2019	ARCHITECTURAL CONCEPT: Ortner und Ortner OPENING: 2001 EXHIBITION AREA: 5,400 m² (58,100 sq ft) over 5 floors

MUSEUM	MEASUREMENT DATE	ROOMS MEASURED	EXHIBITIONS AT TIME OF MEASUREMENT	BASIC INFO ON THE MUSEUM'S ARCHITECTURE
ALBERTINA, VIENNA	2 Jun 2016	Random sampling	*Erwin Bohatsch* 8 Apr–12 Jun 2016 *Land & Leute aus der Fotosammlung der Albertina* 25 May–8 Oct 2016 *Anselm Kiefer, die Holzschnitte* 18 Mar–19 June 2016	Refurbishment & expansion ARCHITECTURE: Erich G. Steinmayr Friedrich H. Mascher Hans Hollein Arkan Zeytinoglu RE-OPENING: 2002
GEORG KARGL FINE ARTS (GALLERY), VIENNA	2 Jun 2016	Random sampling	Herwig Turk *LINESCAPE* 13 May–30 Jul 2016 Nedko Solakov *STORIES* 13 May–30 Jul 201	FOUNDED: 1998 EXHIBITION AREA: 350 m² (3,760 sq. ft)
GALERIE THOMAN, VIENNA	2 Jun 2016	Random sampling	*Julia Bornefeld morphic fields* 12 May–27 Aug 2016	None
KUNSTHAUS BREGENZ (KUB)	29 Sep 2022 (3:30 –6:00 p.m.)	Ground floor and 2nd floor	*Jordan Wolfson* 16 Jul–09 Oct 2022	ARCHITECTURE: Peter Zumthor CONSTRUCTION: 1990–1997 USABLE AREA: 3,340 m² (35,950 sq ft) EXHIBITION AREA: 450 m² (4,840 sq ft) EACH FLOOR: 1,800 m² (19,370 sq ft)

△ Table 6. List of surveyed museums

During the measurement process, the spectrometer's user interface allowed me to select which data were displayed from among four optional screen displays (BASIC/SPECTRUM/CIE1931/CIE1976), and it was possible to change views while measuring. I chose the spectrum setting to begin with. It was fascinating to note the vastly different spectra between the various museums; even when there was some commonality—in color temperature and illuminance, for example—the spectral imaging usually appeared quite different. My main focus with the first measurements was therefore exclusively on the spectral images. Figure 19 shows selected results—the striking differences can be seen clearly. The measurement results recorded in these spectral analyses were used for Case Study 03, during which the test subjects could see a display of light-measurement data for each respective space.

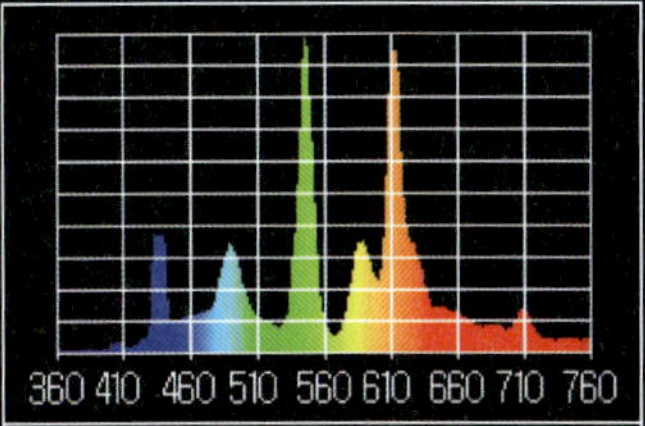

M1

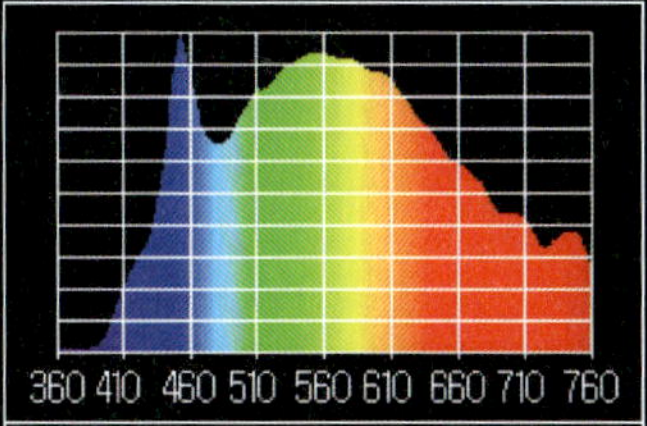

M2

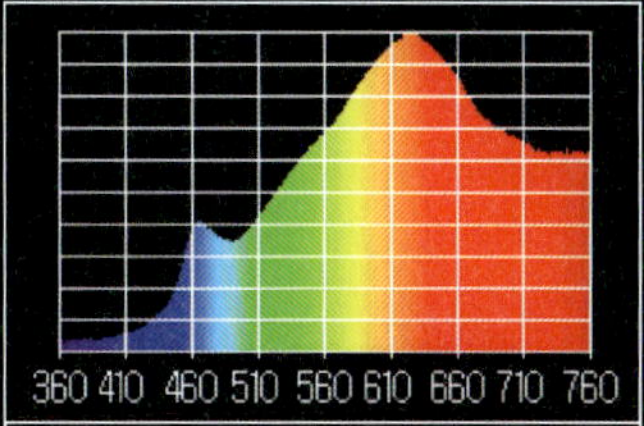

M3

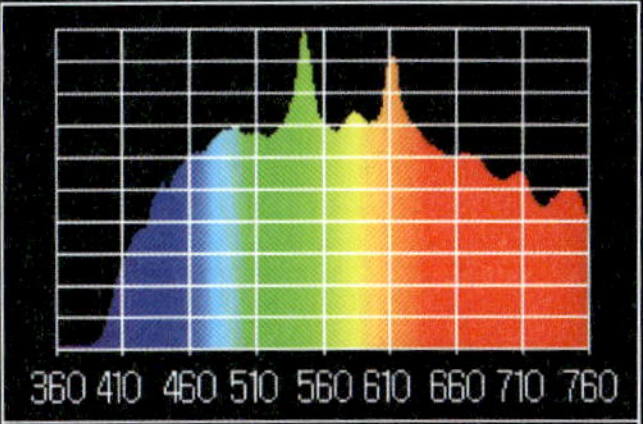

M6

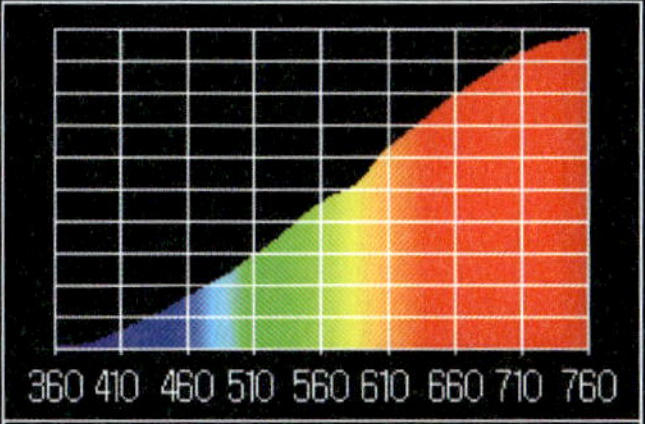

M9

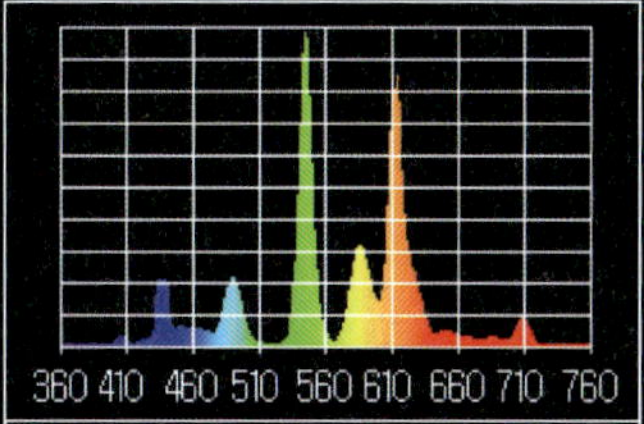

M10

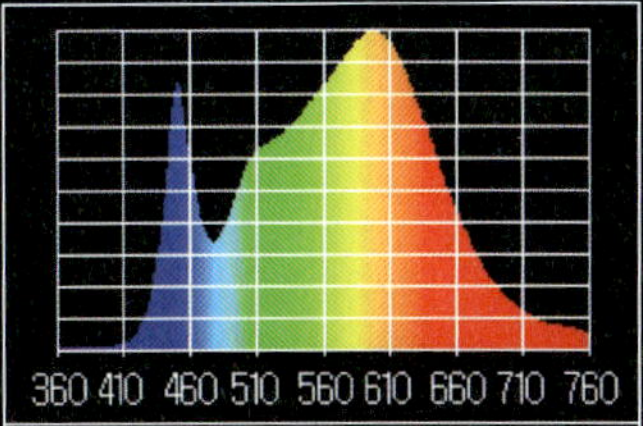

M12

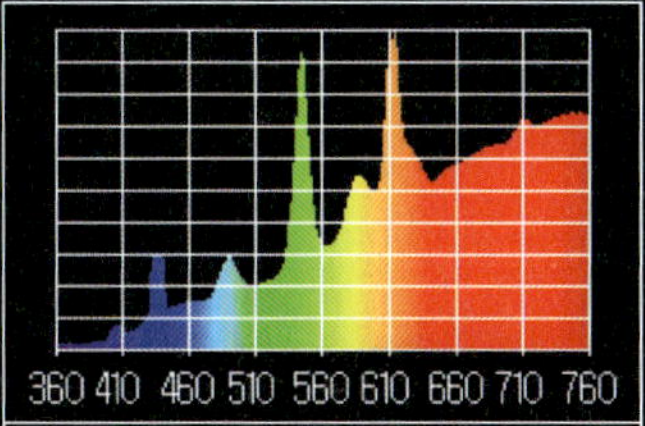

M13

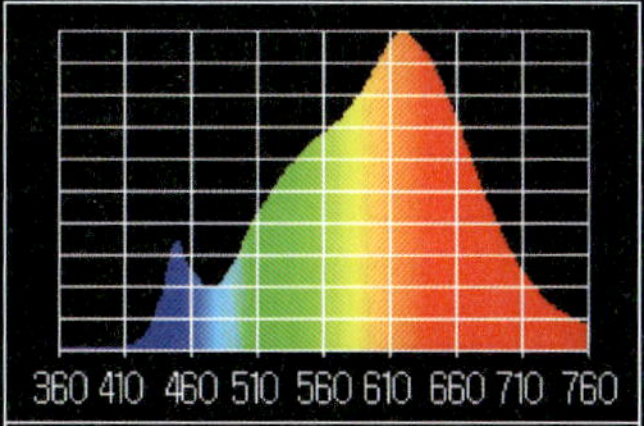

M15

While conducting these light surveys in the museums listed above, I kept notes on my observations. Here are a few unedited excerpts that give some insight into the process of surveying the buildings and rooms.

29 MARCH 2017: MUMOK, VIENNA

The significant difference between the lighting conditions in the circulation areas and those inside the exhibition spaces was striking. When you enter mumok, daylight follows you into the 35-meter-high (115-feet-high) foyer, flooding the lofty space from above. Bridges connecting different exhibition levels are reached via centrally located glass elevators.

Light measurements began in the large gallery on the top floor—the only exhibition space in the museum where daylight comes into play. It enters the room through a large opening in the arched ceiling and through panoramic windows. All other galleries are artificially illuminated. Therefore, except for the top floor survey, the measurements exclusively represent the qualities of artificial lighting. The rooms were measured in sequence, from the top to the bottom floors. The measurements took place under the supervision of a museum security officer.

The lighting conditions in the exhibition spaces stood in contrast with the daylight in the circulation areas between them. I found the repeated shifting contrast between daylight and artificial light to be quite a strain on the eyes. The lighting conditions in the various exhibition spaces were nearly identical. Most of the lighting came from recessed ceiling fixtures, with one exception: the small gallery on level 2 was already outfitted with LED spots.

7 APRIL 2017: SECESSION, VIENNA

At the time of the lighting measurement, the main gallery, one of the very first White Cubes ever built, was illuminated by daylight filtering into the room through the glass ceiling. The light distribution left a very balanced impression. The measurements revealed a very uniform overall picture. The spectral images displayed a very nice and complete spectrum, similar to the daylight's, which suggested a high CRI value. In fact, the color-rendering value was below 90 CRI in all measurements. These results indicate that the quality of light in the exhibition space is determined by the artificial light sources installed in the space above the glass ceiling. It should be noted here that these measurement results were obtained before a general renovation in 2018 by the architect Adolf Krischanitz, who replaced the fluorescent tubes installed above the glass ceiling in the 1980s with Tunable White LEDs. Presently, the color temperature can be steplessly adjusted between 3,000 K to 6,000 K and thus adapted to the natural daylight.

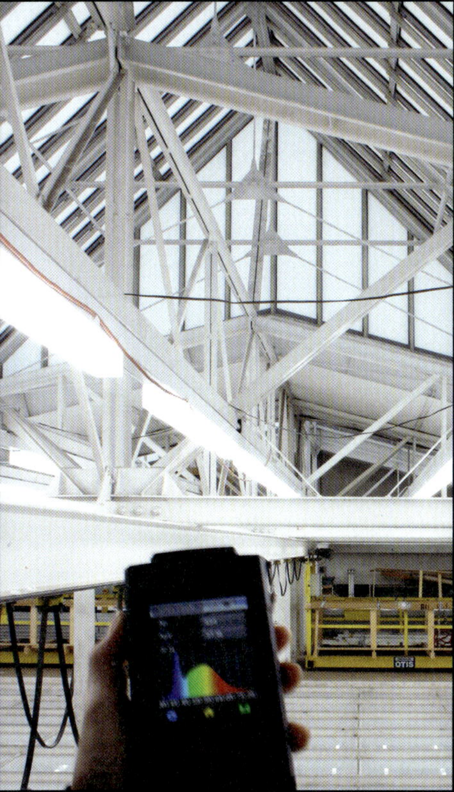
OTIS

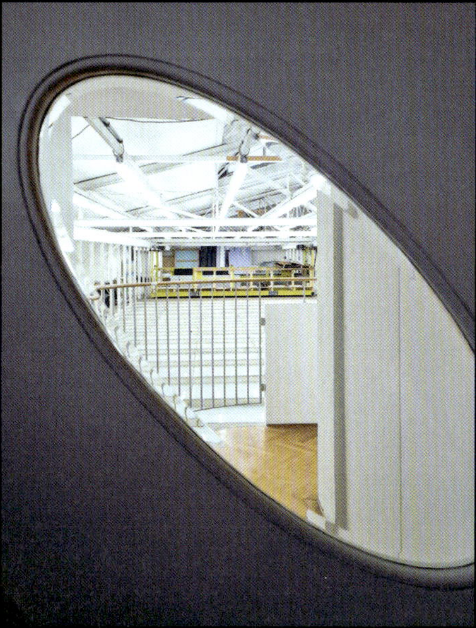

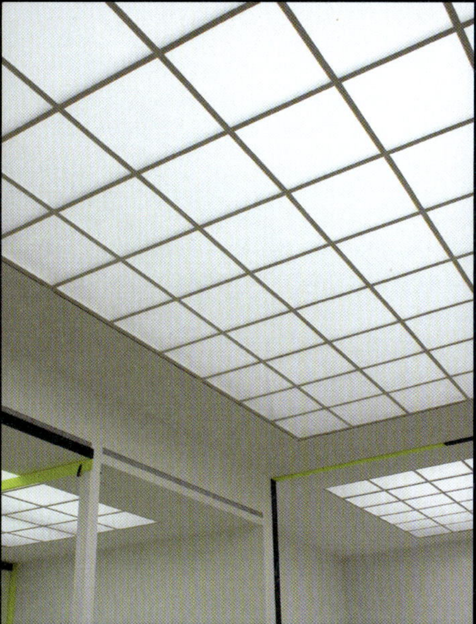

30 JUNE 2017: MAK, VIENNA

The ground-floor exhibition hall and the basement design lab are two very different White Cubes. Both rooms are only used for temporary exhibitions.

The exhibition space of the design lab is characterized by the exposed-concrete ceiling beams. This room is nearly quadratic. Here, a track lighting system has been installed along the ceiling grid. For the exhibition on at the time of the measurement, various track spotlights with different color temperatures were in use. It's not possible to say if this was intended by the designers. I couldn't notice any significant correlation between the color temperatures chosen and the artwork on display.

In the large exhibition hall, track spotlights were mounted at regular intervals along the lines of power rails. For the most part, they were aimed at the walls. Like the Kunsthistorisches Museum, this exhibition hall had originally allowed daylight via its glass ceiling. The MAK's skylight is now completely opaque and retrofitted with recessed ceiling lights.

12 AUGUST 2017: LENTOS, LINZ

The temporary exhibition areas and the second-story rooms displaying the permanent collection are spanned by one continuous glass ceiling that filters daylight into the space. Artificial lamps are built into the ceiling and switched on depending on the prevailing daylight conditions. The light changes according to time of day and the weather. How it changes when the sky is overcast is shown by the comparison of two measurement results (see fig. 21). The differences are visible in the spectral images as well as in the values for illuminance and color rendering. For example, the illuminance increases from 123 to 217 lux.

On the top floor of the museum special attention is given to the quality of lighting displayed. I did not find comparable conditions in the basement, where the quality of artificial lighting stands in stark contrast to the upper floor.

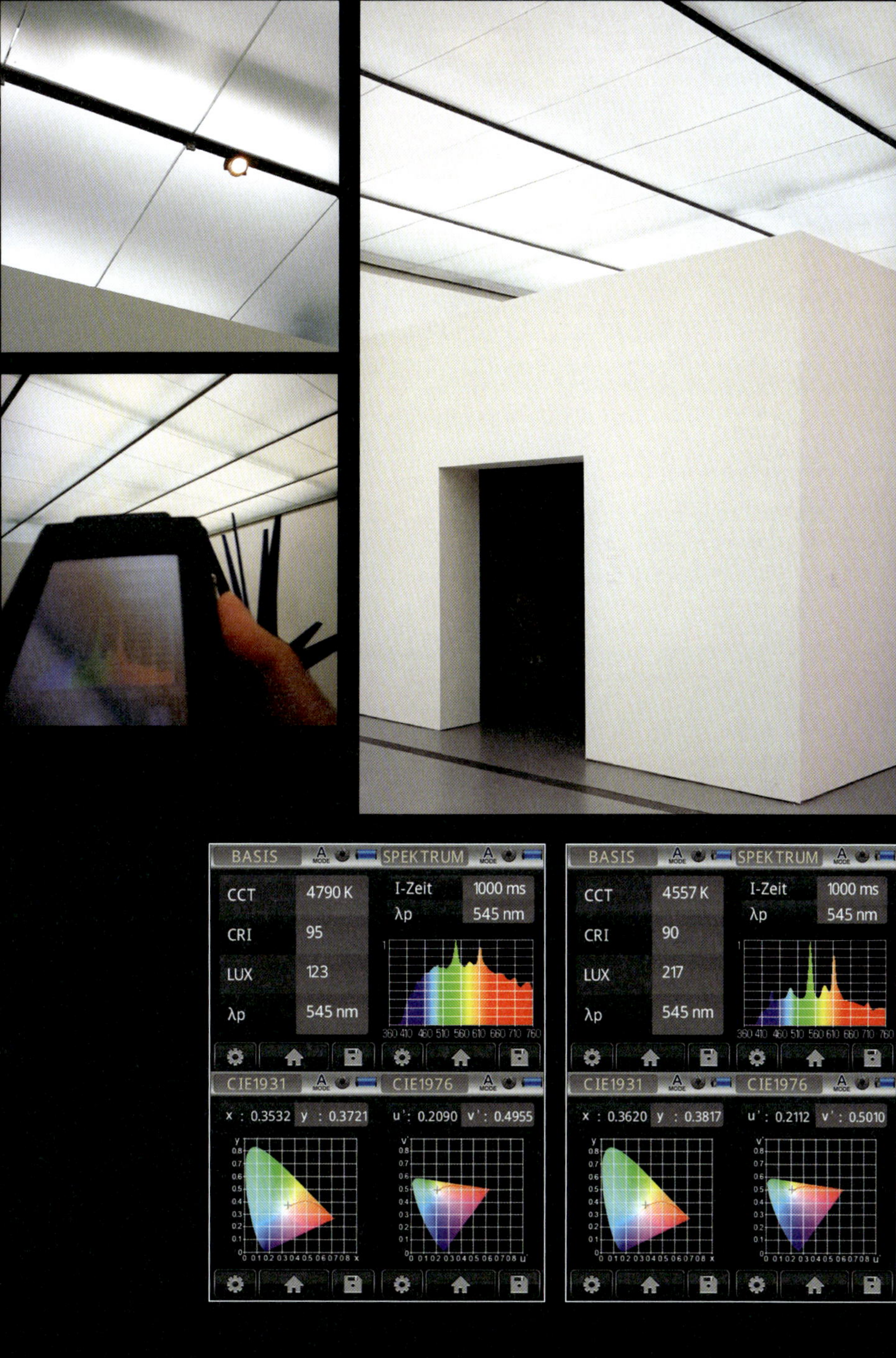

△ Figure 21. Photo gallery: ceiling light and lighting measurements compari clear *(left)* and overcast skies *(right)*, 12 December 2017, Lentos, Linz, top floor

12 AUGUST 2017: MUSEUM DER MODERNE, SALZBURG

This museum's lighting reminds me of the lighting at mumok. I spoke with a gallery attendant and learned that she and her colleagues find the prevailing artificial lighting conditions stressful and fatiguing. They regularly take their breaks in the areas where daylight enters the building. As in mumok, the common access area is naturally lit from above. The qualities of the natural light and artificial light were strikingly different.

9 NOVEMBER 2017: KUNSTFORUM, VIENNA

In general, I tried to take the light measurements as objectively as possible and let myself critique the exhibition spaces only as I'm wrapping up my measurements. In the Kunstforum, I found this approach relatively difficult. From the start, the lighting seemed dull to me, rendering the rooms lifeless and monotonous.

14 NOVEMBER 2017: RAINER MUSEUM, BADEN BEI WIEN

This museum is a landmarked building that was originally designed to be a thermal spa for ladies. Its exhibition spaces are not White Cubes, in the classic sense. The individual rooms also differ from one another in terms of construction materials and size. Nevertheless, the lighting concept in this museum is very interesting, as the daylight entering from side windows plays a key role. The lighting conditions vary with the course of daylight. Due to the mixture of artificial and natural lighting, the measurement results display wide fluctuations in luminous intensity, color temperatures and Color Rendering Index. Arnulf Rainer's richly colored artworks are afforded multifaceted qualities due to changing light conditions throughout the day.

24 NOVEMBER 2017: KUNSTHALLE WIEN, VIENNA

While I took light readings in the Kunsthalle Wien, it was the first time I was able to see evidence that merely a few lux can provide complete information about the DNA of light. The room on the upper floor was completely darkened for the current exhibition and only single lamps were used to target specific objects with light. One lux was sufficient to obtain usable results and to create a complete spectral image. An employee of the Kunsthalle drew my attention to the fact that in the basement exhibition room, the lighting for various events can be changed at the touch of a button, and I was able to measure the space's various light settings. The results showed differences in only the luminous intensity.

17 JANUARY 2018: AIL, VIENNA

The exhibition spaces of the AIL (Angewandte Interdisciplinary Lab) were planned and built in 2010 for the BAWAG Contemporary gallery by the architectural firm propeller z, and are located in the interior ground floor and basement of a multi story *Gründerzeit* (turn-of-the-century) building. AIL uses the spaces only for temporary exhibitions. The exhibition space in the basement is a classic White Cube illuminated only with fluorescent tube lamps aligned parallel to the longer walls. The exhibition spaces on the ground floor, on the other hand, are dominated by the large floor-to-ceiling glass walls on the street side, as well as the central glass roof. Artificial and natural light are blended here, depending upon the exhibition design. Here, too, fluorescent lamps are installed parallel to the walls. The spaces are uniformly illuminated. There is no lighting specifically targeting the artworks. The lights are not dimmable. The spaces appear very bright—a first impression that is confirmed by the measurements.

7 MARCH 2018: UPPER BELVEDERE, VIENNA

The surveys took place under the supervision of a museum security official. The permanent exhibition space was reconceived in early 2018 and reopened in March. The light measurements were made room by room according to standard procedure. Some of the exhibition walls were covered in fabric. The Belvedere palace allows daylight to enter sideways through the windows. However, all artworks are illuminated exclusively by artificial lighting, which is what was measured. Especially interesting was the light staging in the Medieval room. The entire room was dark, with black walls. The exposure reading was only one lux and the lighting was targeted directly onto the pictures, giving them a glowing appearance, almost as if they were video screens.

MARCH 2018: BELVEDERE 21, VIENNA

During my measurements, all windows of Belvedere 21 were darkened with curtains, which is quite unusual for this museum, where daylight normally plays a feature role. The light fixtures (fluorescent) are mounted flat on the ceiling. The second-floor rooms were also darkened, therefore the measurements for this museum are exclusively taken under artificial lighting.

Note: Rachel Whiteread's sculptures made of epoxy resin are apparently quite sensitive to daylight. Her work is exhibited exclusively under artificial lighting, also at Tate Modern in London. Dynamic artificial lighting would be ideal for these sculptures.

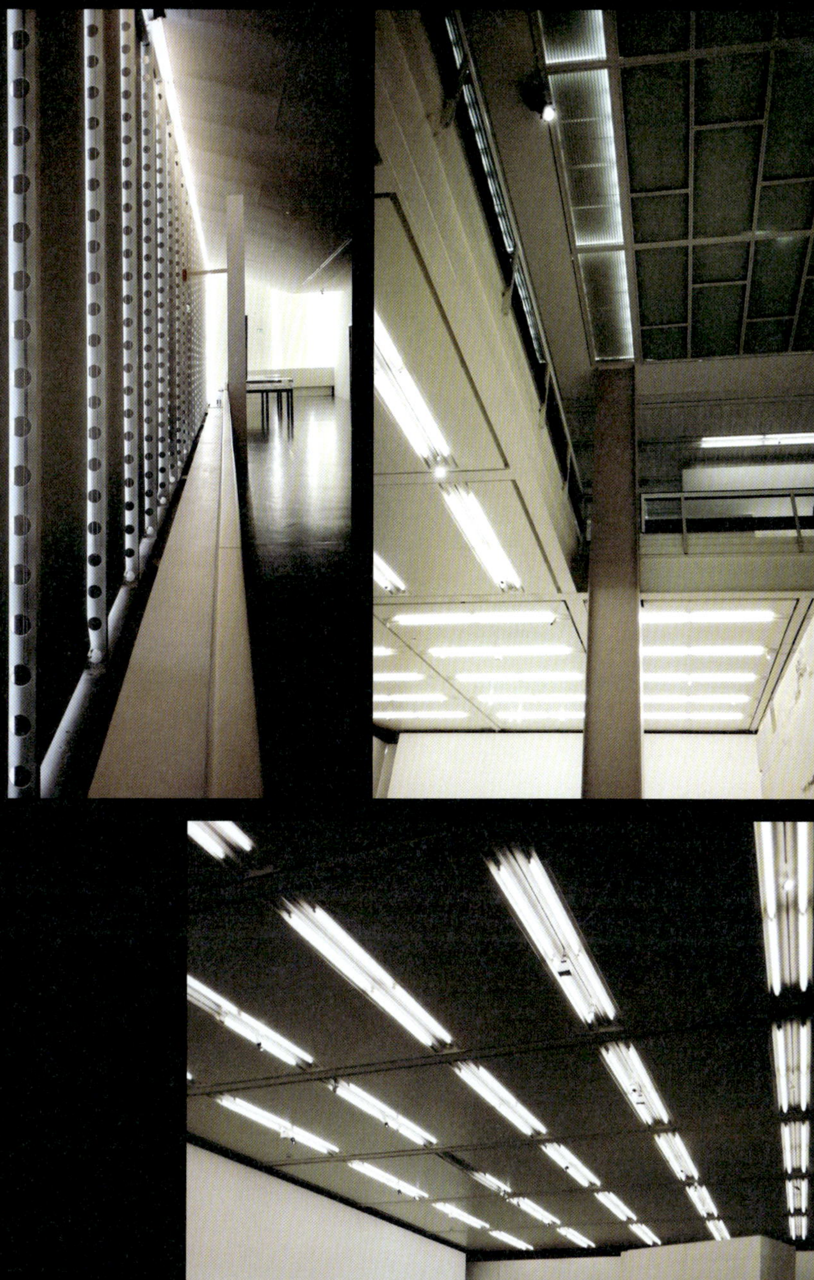

△ Figure 22. Darkened facade and ceiling lights, Belvedere 21. Museum of Contemporary Art, Vienna

29 SEPTEMBER 2022: KUNSTHAUS BREGENZ (KUB)

Designed by the architect Peter Zumthor, the Kunsthaus Bregenz is illuminated by natural daylight. The museum's architecture remains impressive, even 25 years after its opening.

Light measurements took place in the afternoon. Only the galleries on the ground floor and second floor could be measured, as the first floor was darkened to display a video work and the third floor was inaccessible for measurement due to the exhibition of *Female Figure* (2014) by the artist Jordan Wolfson. The results of measurements taken on the ground floor differ significantly from those taken in the floors above. On the ground floor, daylight filters into the room through the translucent multilayered glass façade and the concrete ceiling determines the character of the room.

The exhibition spaces on the upper stories, on the other hand, are top-lit through glass ceilings, above which a two-meter-high cavity permits light to enter laterally via reflective light bands on all four sides of the etched glass façade. When needed, the 235 pendant lights installed in each floor's cavity can be switched on individually or entirely, and each luminaire is steplessly dimmable.

The measurement results once again show the interdependence between lighting quality and the light source used. As soon as daylight and artificial light are mixed, the quality of the artificial light impacts the overall result significantly. It should be noted here that since the measurements were taken, LED luminaires have been installed during renovations in March 2023.

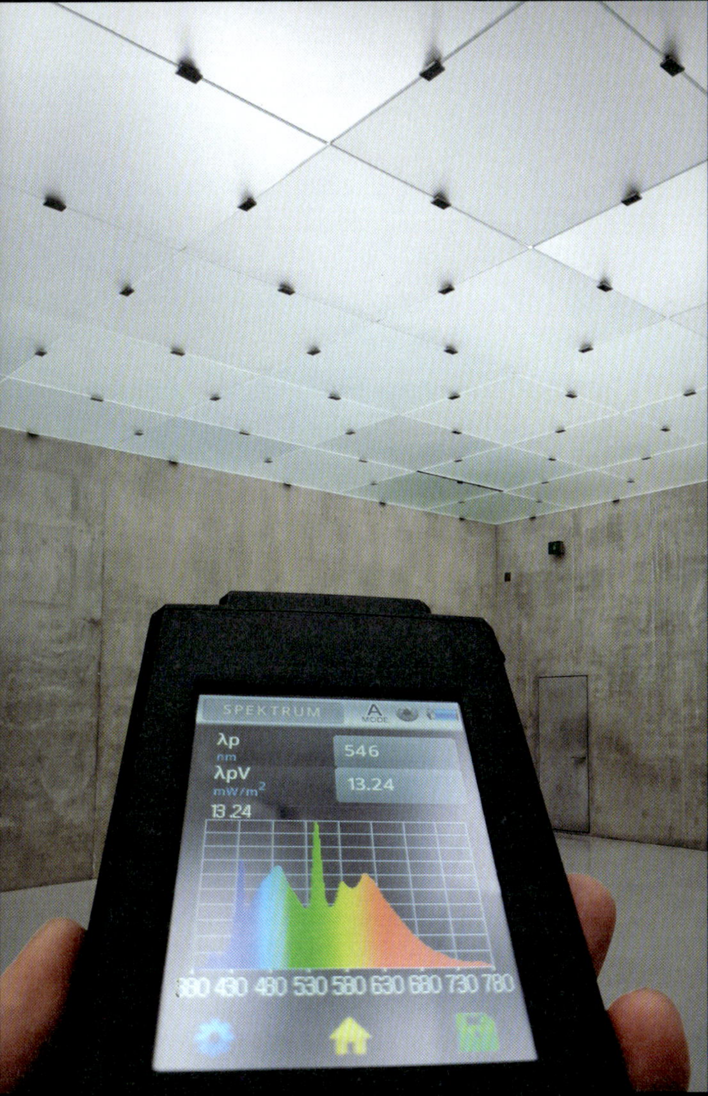

△ Figure 23. Photo of light measurements: Kunsthaus Bregenz (KUB), exhibition space 2nd floor

EVALUATION OF THE MEASUREMENTS

The measurement results were saved as images (BMP) and as spreadsheet data (Excel). The data served as the foundation for the White Cube Teleporter research project that took place in a Viennese pop-up gallery, Raumlabor S3T14, and at the AIL's exhibition space.

The collected measurement results offer an insight into the current lighting conditions of representative museums and galleries in Vienna and Austria.

OVERVIEW OF SELECTED MEASUREMENT RESULTS

MUSEUM	TYPE OF ART	MEASUREMENT DATE (DD.MM.YYYY)	CCT (K)	CRI (R_a)	LUX
04	Classic/Traditional	18.01.2018	3,175	88	66
11	Classic/Traditional	07.03.2018	3,357	92	399
14	Classic/Traditional	30.03.2019	3,290	85	135
02	Pre-modern	07.04.2017	4,838	87	505
08	Pre-modern/Modern	09.11.2017	3,397	91	64
13	Pre-modern/Modern	09.03.2019	3,530	93	281
15	Pre-modern/Modern	13.02.2018	2,980	90	148
06	Modern/Contemporary	12.08.2017	4,824	89	126
07	Modern/Contemporary	12.08.2017	3,618	79	62
12	Modern/Contemporary	07.03.2018	4,192	89	70
01	Contemporary	29.03.2017	3,572	90	50
03	Contemporary	30.06.2017	2,919	95	108
05	Contemporary	17.01.2018	5,328	86	697
09	Contemporary	14.11.2017	3,989	96	195
10	Contemporary	24.11.2017	3,380	81	216

△ Table 7. Overview of the surveyed museums and their (averaged) measurement values

Since lighting technologies are constantly changing and museums and galleries are also regularly retrofitted, the results shown are snapshots. Researchers from the Empirical Visual Aesthetics Labs (EVAlab) at the University of Vienna collaborated on the data analysis. Exhibition venues were categorized as exhibitors of traditional art, modern art and/or contemporary art in the course of Case Study 01. Trends emerge when the results are grouped according to these individual categories.

In table 7, the names of the institutions have been deliberately omitted, because the purpose of evaluating the data is solely to create an overall picture, not to assess the lighting conditions of any specific institution. The table illustrates a nice cross-section of lighting conditions and plainly demonstrates that art illumination of various museums and galleries is strikingly inconsistent.

The color-rendering (CRI) value ranges from 79 R_a to 96 R_a. The lowest color temperature is 2,919 K and the highest is 5,328 K. When the data are grouped into their respective categories, it becomes apparent that traditional art is usually displayed under warm color temperatures, whereas modern and contemporary art are exhibited under quite varied color temperatures. A wide variance is also found with measurements of luminous intensity; here, they range between 50 and 697 lux and, as Kruithof suggested, there is a correlation between the measured lux and CRI values. Lower lux values tend to be found in the museums with lower color temperatures and higher lux values in the museums with higher color temperatures.

WHITE CUBE TELEPORTER— A THREE-PHASE RESEARCH PROJECT

Dynamic artificial lighting makes it possible to reproduce the lighting characteristics of individual museums in the experimental laboratory. The core findings in this book stem from the White Cube Teleporter research project. Dynamic artificial lighting was explored as a design tool in a space that was as neutral as possible: the White Cube. As an architect, my goal for this series of experiments was to evaluate the potential for dynamic artificial lighting of art exhibitions and to get artists involved in this discussion. The White Cube Teleporter research project took place between January 2016 and June 2019 and was carried out in different phases.

PHASE 1

Test Run A:	Evaluating the interaction between light setting and artwork
Case Study 01:	Does gallery lighting really have an impact on art appreciation? (empirical study)
Test Run B:	*One Artist / Two White Cubes / Five Museums* (exhibition)

PHASE 2

Case Study 02:	*Five Artists × Five Museums* (exhibition)

PHASE 3

Case Study 03:	*Lighthouse* (installation/exhibition)

The research activities (fig. 24) included three case studies that took place within different experimental settings and spaces.

Case Study 01 took place in a facsimile of a White Cube (in a building on Herrengasse, in Vienna's city center). Case Study 02 and Case Study 03 were carried out in the White Cube at Vienna's AIL (Angewandte Interdisciplinary Lab).

BASELINE STUDY (BENCHMARKING)

- Survey of existing exhibition spaces

RESEARCH LOCATIONS → 3-PHASE PROCESS

SPACE 1
RAUMLABOR S3T14

2 REPLICAS OF WHITE CUBES
2 LIGHTCUBES

Apr 2017–Jan 2018

- Covering up windows
- Concept for artificial light sources
- Installation of Lightcubes
- Testing of white wall paint (reflectance of spectral components of the artificial lighting)
- Selection of artworks
- Programming the lighting system

SPACE 2
RAUMLABOR S3T14

1 ACTUAL WHITE CUBE
2 LIGHTCUBES

Feb 2018–Jun 2019

- Installation of Lightcubes
- Programming the lighting system based on measured benchmarks
- Selection of artworks
- Design of the walls / exhibition design
- Design and programming of dynamic-lighting sequences

PHASE 1

TEST RUN A

Testing the effects between light settings and artwork using the series *Spectrum 2016* in preparation for Case Study 02

CASE STUDY 01

Does gallery lighting really have an impact on appreciation of art? (empirical study in cooperation with the University of Vienna's Empirical Visual Aesthetics Labs*)

TEST RUN B

One Artist / Two White Cubes / Five Museums

Test the setting of a public exhibition in preparation for Case Study 02

PHASE 2

CASE STUDY 02

Research in a real exhibition space

Part 1: Test setting for the exhibition *Five Artists × Five Museums*

PHASE 3

CASE STUDY 03

Research in a real exhibition space

Part 2: *Lighthouse*—an experimental exhibition dealing with the potential of dynamic lighting

* Empirical Visual Aesthetics Labs, Faculty of Psychology, Department of Basic Psychological Research and Research Methods, University of Vienna, Austria

△ Figure 24. Schematic diagram: sequence of research activities

All case studies used "Lightcubes"—a mobile lighting system designed specifically for this purpose (see page 142). This made it possible to replicate the lighting conditions of existing exhibition spaces within the test setting, as well as to program and play back new dynamic-lighting sequences.

CASE STUDY 01

Case Study 01 examined the effect different museums' light settings have on art appreciation. Here, a special focus was on color temperature. In the course of the study, which was conducted jointly with the University of Vienna's Department of Cognition, Emotion, and Methods in Psychology, the test subjects were allowed to choose their preferred color temperature in a second step. On display were three paintings (portraits of women painted around 1900) from the collection of the University of Applied Arts Vienna, as well as three abstract paintings by the artist Friedrich Biedermann. The results of this study were revealed in an academic article published jointly with the University of Vienna (Pelowski, Leder, Graser et al. 2019).

CASE STUDY 02

Case Study 02 was executed as an exhibition that included five artworks by five contemporary artists, displayed to the public under five different lighting conditions. The question was: *with* what light and *for* what light was the art created, and *under* what light should it be presented to the audience? The point of this case study was to place the experimental test setup into a real exhibition context, and to use dynamic artificial lighting to form a dialogue between the artists and the audience. In addition to color temperature, the Color Rendering Index also played a key role here, as this reveals how similar artificial lighting is to natural light (sunlight has a color-rendering value of 100 R_a, the maximum value on the CRI scale). The audience became an active part of the experiment in Case Study 02. For one of the five artworks, viewers could press a button to select one of five light settings replicating those in actual museums. The remaining four artworks were illuminated dynamically; the lighting changed automatically every 20 seconds through a cycle of five settings, lasting 100 seconds in total. Quite different artworks were deliberately selected in order to examine the effect of lighting on our visual perception of contemporary art. At the same time, this enabled a testing setup that explored the potential of dynamic artificial lighting.

CASE STUDY 03

For Case Study 03, an exhibition was conceived together with the artist Friedrich Biedermann built upon the results of the previous experiments. In our respective roles as architect and artist, we examined the potential of dynamic lighting as a design tool deployed in a White Cube. The light settings took into account color temperature, color-rendering value, luminous intensity and spectrum. The art, the space and the audience formed a pattern of relationships through the intermediary of light. A portion of this installation was subsequently shown at the summer 2019 exhibition, *Understanding Art & Research*, at Vienna's Museum of Applied Arts.

DESIGN OF THE RESEARCH SPACE–WHITE CUBE

I chose the White Cube as the launch pad for my research—a decision that I made ostensibly for architectural considerations unconnected to its art-historical context as an exhibition space. In other words, it was rather a matter of choosing a minimalist space that would allow light to take center stage. My choice was influenced by theorist Brian O'Doherty's specifications for a White Cube's configuration: white walls, a dark floor and illuminated ceiling, all *artificially illuminated* (cf. O'Doherty 1976/1986: 10). Another reason for my decision was the White Cube's *room specifications* and *functional program*, in the architectural sense of defining a space. Functioning as an exhibition space, the White Cube provides the characteristics necessary for analyzing the effects of light in architecture. It is a space that I, as a beholder, absorb with all my senses, and visual perception plays a key role. It is a space that I can experience physically—its simple geometry can be easily discerned and it becomes a setting for the ambience that develops within it.

SELECTION OF LIGHTING TECHNOLOGY—PiLED

For the art-based research project, White Cube Teleporter, PiLED lighting technology was used because it satisfied the required characteristics and capacities. Light-emitting diode (LED) technology was selected upon the premise that current development of LED-based digital lighting technologies is steadily advancing, and with the expectation that LED technologies will allow us to customize lighting design. Despite the fact that the light quality from earlier LED technology left much to be desired, we are convinced that today's LEDs are up to the task. The white light produced by today's LEDs comes close to the ideal of natural daylight. The new generation of LEDs offers, among other things, a high Color Rendering Index, a continuous spectrum and variable color temperatures. Human Centric Lighting (HCL) technologies simulate the course of daylight, while innovative controller systems allow us to individually program and control dynamic-lighting systems.

The PiLED is a state-of-the-art, three-channel LED technology (see pages 84–89) allowing a perfect calibration of the illuminant, as well as stepless control. This choice was not about focusing on any one particular product, but to use the one that is forward-looking and would generate seminal test results.

PROCESS OF THE RESEARCH PROJECT

For all our studies, extracted data from the measurements of surveyed exhibition spaces served as benchmarks for reproducing their respective lighting conditions in the research spaces. The goal was to examine the effect different lighting conditions have on the perception of art and to raise awareness of this effect among the viewers. Assuming that dynamic artificial lighting will impact museums in the near future, we examined questions concerning which lighting for art is preferred by viewers, and under which lighting the artist intended his or her work to be presented. These are questions relevant to museum architects, exhibition designers, curators and artists, because we make the decisions about the lighting moods for exhibition spaces and how the art is illuminated.

As art museums and galleries are typically open to the public, our research facilities for all three case studies were conceived as public exhibition spaces. Case Studies 02 and 03 were experiments adhering to the rules of artistic research, in contrast to the empirical nature of Case Study 01. In both cases, art exhibitions were mounted that directly involved the audience and turned the viewers into test subjects. The results of Case Study 01 were published accordingly in October 2019 (see Pelowski, Leder, Graser et al. 2019).

Case Study 01 is only one part of the whole project. Despite different depths of analysis across all three case studies, they will henceforth be given equal weight so that conclusions can be inferred. In the end, after all, all three case studies focus on the potential of dynamic lighting in art museums.

For Case Study 01, facsimiles of two gallery spaces were created and the lighting replicated the conditions of the previously surveyed exhibition spaces. The artwork could thus be viewed under the various light conditions of existing museums. Rather than lighting the artwork directly, the walls of the White Cube were homogeneously illuminated, so that the room conveyed a uniform lighting ambience. The lighting technology we used was not selected primarily for being human-centric, but mainly because it offered us the possibility to recreate artificial and natural lighting conditions at the push of a button. It also offered the possibility to interactively engage in the artistic creative process as well as in the exhibition process. The lighting became a communicator, taking on a mediating role.

But how can we measure the impact of lighting on one's perception of art? Seeking to answer this question, I started a dialogue with the physicist and light expert, Prof. Günther Leising, and the perception researcher, Prof. Helmut Leder. In cooperation with the Empirical Visual Aesthetics Labs of the University of Vienna, the setting for Case Study 01 was established in October 2017. To a lesser extent, we also explored the nonvisual perception of light by asking the test subjects how they felt while viewing the art. Because the HCL technology used in this study was mainly static, the pictures viewed during each test round were displayed under a specific, fixed light setting. Therefore, no conclusions could be drawn on the impact of light, in terms of HCL research.

Interestingly, however, the results of our study indicate that there may be an emotional connection between the lighting and the art on display. Warm light was preferred for abstract art and cold light for figurative art.

The individual's subjective preference about which lighting is best was shown by the wide variance of results in the second round, during which the test subjects were allowed to autonomously choose the color temperature for viewing art. The results ranged between very cold and very warm light. The results of the study corroborated the psychologists' hypothesis that people are able to adapt very quickly to different lighting conditions and that the light factor does not play such a critical role in the perception of art (cf. Pelowski, Leder, Graser et al. 2019).

In the course of our further research activities, however, we were indeed able to discover how differently the images appear under different light settings, and we incorporated these findings into the subsequent experiments. Following the study, the facsimile gallery spaces created in a private apartment building on Vienna's Herrengasse were opened up to the general public as an exhibition. This was the first chance I had to expose a wider audience to a White Cube under dynamic lighting. The public could now view the art under different light settings, in contrast to the study, where a static light setting was chosen for each round of tests and which only gave us the ability to adjust the light from one round to the next at the push of a button. Based on this experience, we developed the concept for carrying out Case Study 02 in the gallery spaces of the AIL (Angewandte Interdisciplinary Lab).

Following the Herrengasse experience, our second major study, Case Study 02, was carried out in the form of an exhibition titled *Five Artists × Five Museums*. As its title suggests, five works by five artists were displayed under lighting conditions that simulated those in five different existing museums. The AIL's basement exhibition space was a typical White Cube. During the exhibition's 14-day run, artists and art enthusiasts could actively choose from among the five different light settings for viewing the artwork. The rectangular room was illuminated as two separate square areas. In the first half of the room, a Lightcube equipped with four spotlights on each side could be controlled manually by visitors via a tablet controller. In the back half of the room, a second Lightcube was automatically controlled according to a dynamic lighting sequence of five different light settings that changed automatically within a specified timeframe. The transitions were abrupt. Each museum's static lighting setting was represented sequentially.

In our third and final experiment—Case Study 03—both light sources (Lightcubes) were used in tandem and lighting became a dynamic design tool within the White Cube. An exhibition titled *Lighthouse* (AIL, 3 March–3 April 2019), was conceived in collaboration with artist Friedrich Biedermann. In the center of the room, a floating sculpture (also named *Lighthouse*) was hung from the ceiling. The walls were graphically designed in black-and-white patterns. Light functioned as the glue that unites art, space and viewer. The light settings were programmed to match the values measured at the surveyed museums and they changed automatically at fixed time intervals. The transitions were gradual—the whole range of lighting conditions measured at each existing museum was deployed, not only its averaged result.

S3T14: INTERDISCIPLINARY LIGHT MEASUREMENT

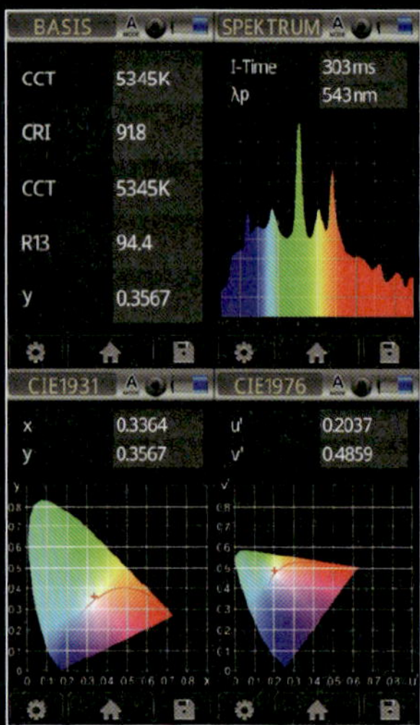

GALLERY I

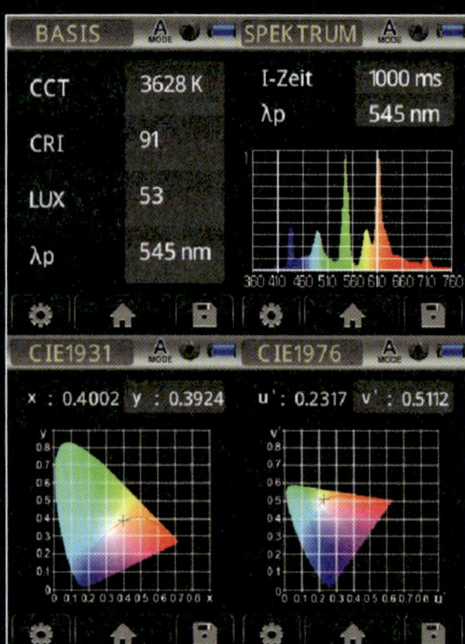

MUSEUM II

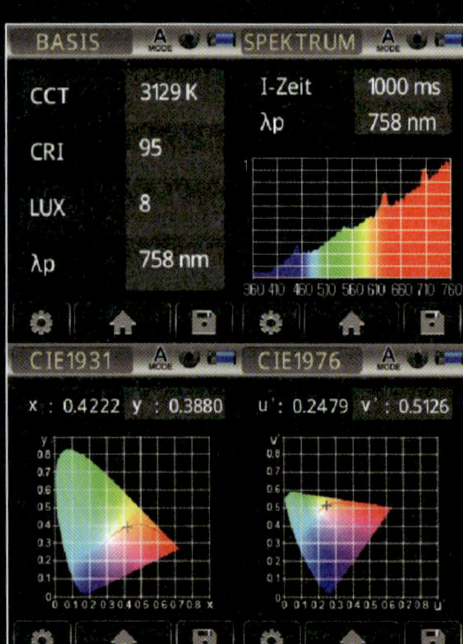

MUSEUM III

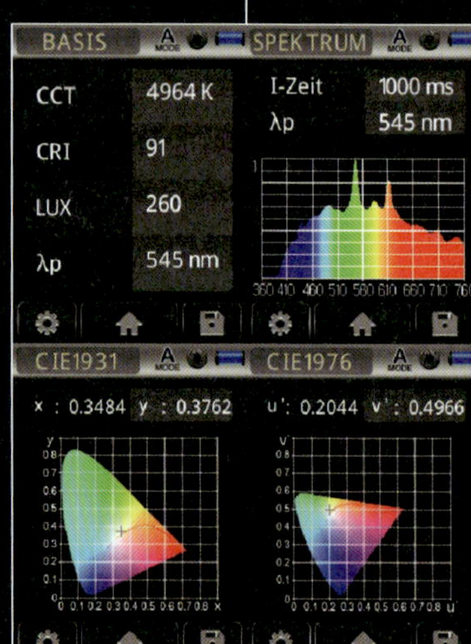

MUSEUM IV

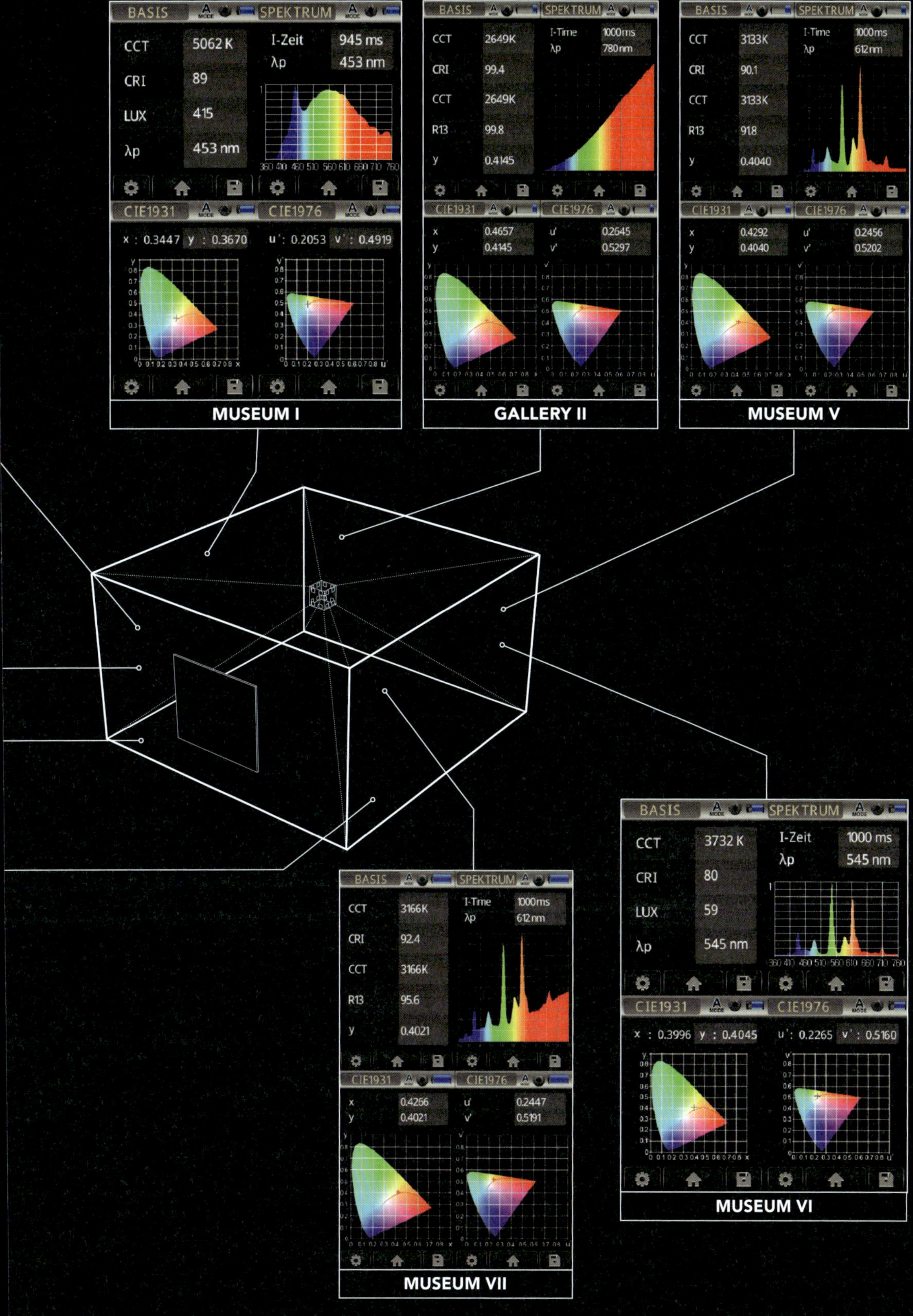

△ Figure 25. White Cube Teleporter, reproduction of selected lighting conditions of existing exhibtion spaces within the setting of a White Cube

PHASE 01: TRIAL RUN A, CASE STUDY 01, TRIAL RUN B

The initial test series, Case Study 01 and the exhibition *One Artist / Two White Cubes / Five Museums* took place in satellite research spaces rented by the University of Applied Arts Vienna and its Institute of Architecture. The research rooms were made available to us from May 2017 to January 2018 and were open to the public. The approximately 110-square-meter (1,180-square-feet) space was located in a residential and office complex (Herrengasse 6–8, Vienna city center) and was subdivided into three rooms, an anteroom, and WC. It was the perfect location for a pop-up gallery, as the university had previously used different spaces there for temporary exhibitions, so it was already familiar within Vienna's art scene.

SETTING UP THE RESEARCH SPACE—RAUMLABOR S3T14

For the research project, the first two rooms (Room A and Room B) were converted into two White Cubes (as shown in the floor plan, fig. 26) and were given the ambience of a small art gallery.

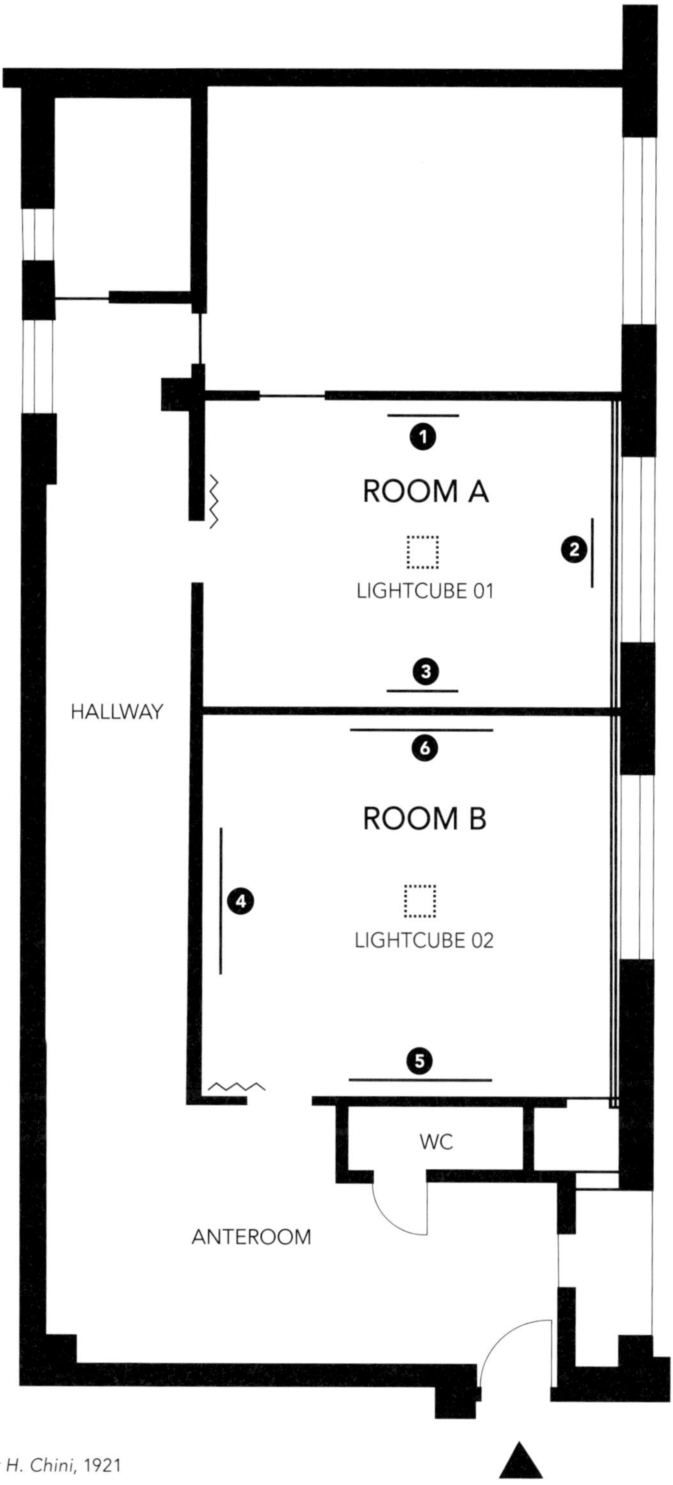

1. Hans Strohofer, *Portrait H. Chini*, 1921
2. Emil Orlik, Untitled portrait of a woman, 1905
3. Ernst Nepo, Untitled portrait of a young girl, c. 1930
4. Friedrich Biedermann, *kar_mu_tho_spectrum*, 2016
5. Friedrich Biedermann, *tho_alb_black_spectrum*, 2016
6. Friedrich Biedermann, *mu_sez_tho_spectrum*, 2016

△ Figure 26. Floorplan of Raumlabor S3T14

Room A encompassed an area measuring 215 square feet (~13 × 16 feet) and Room B had a floor area of 270 square feet (~16 × 16 feet). Both rooms were completely sealed off from natural light and equipped with artificial illuminants. The window openings in both rooms were completely fitted with wood panels, spackled smooth and painted white, as were the walls and ceilings. The white paint was tested for its reflective properties at the Institut für Festkörperphysik (Institute of Solid-State Physics) at the Graz University of Technology under the direction of Prof. Günther Leising. Seven products from five manufacturers were selected for analysis (see table 8).

SELECTION OF TESTED WHITE PAINTS

PAINT	MANUFACTURER	PRODUCT NAME
01	StoColor	Rapid Ultramatt
02	StoColor	Titanium
03	T-Sefra	Blütenweiß
04	T-Sefra	Brillantweiß
05	Adler	Ultraweiß
06	Farrow & Ball	All White 2005
07	Brillux	Super Latex Elf 3000 Weiss

△ Table 8. Overview of white-paint product selections

Based on the measurement results, the decision was made to use Rapid Ultramatt paint from the manufacturer STO, because the drop-off below 420 nm was less pronounced with this paint compared with the other products (see fig. 28).

△ Figure 27. White paint samples

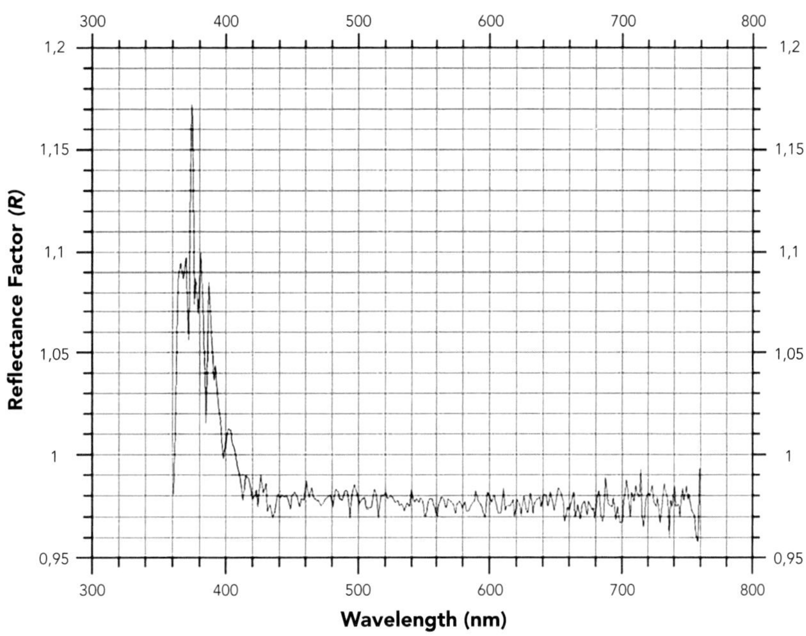

△ Figure 28. Graph showing the reflectance factors of Rapid Ultramatt wall paint over a range of light wavelengths

In Room B, the existing white epoxy resin floor was painted gray (Adler concrete paint Betongrau RAL 70239), while the existing parquet flooring in Room A was left as is, resulting in two different White Cubes. Both interior spaces are common in actual galleries, so we were able to address two different real-space scenarios. It stood to reason to exhibit the contemporary artist's abstract paintings in Room B (concrete floor). Three portraits from the archival collection of the University of Applied Arts Vienna were exhibited in Room A.

DEVELOPMENT AND CONCEPTION OF THE LIGHTING SYSTEM

Together with Prof. Günther Leising, two luminaires were developed for the research project. They were conceived as temporary modular fixtures requiring only one power connection, similar to pendant lighting, and thus deployable in any space. The luminaire's individual spotlights could be individually directed. The individual 12-watt spots were angled at 50° each producing color temperature of 1,800 K to 16,000 K (LED Module PiLED). They were mounted, evenly spaced apart, in bespoke aluminum-frame fixtures measuring approximately one cubic foot (30 cm^3). Both exhibition spaces in the pop-up gallery Raumlabor S3T14 were each equipped with such a Lightcube (see fig. 29). Natural lighting was also blocked out in the vestibule and hallway, which were illuminated from the existing fixtures fitted with two 10-watt Ledon LEDs (E27), emitting a color temperature of 2,700 K.

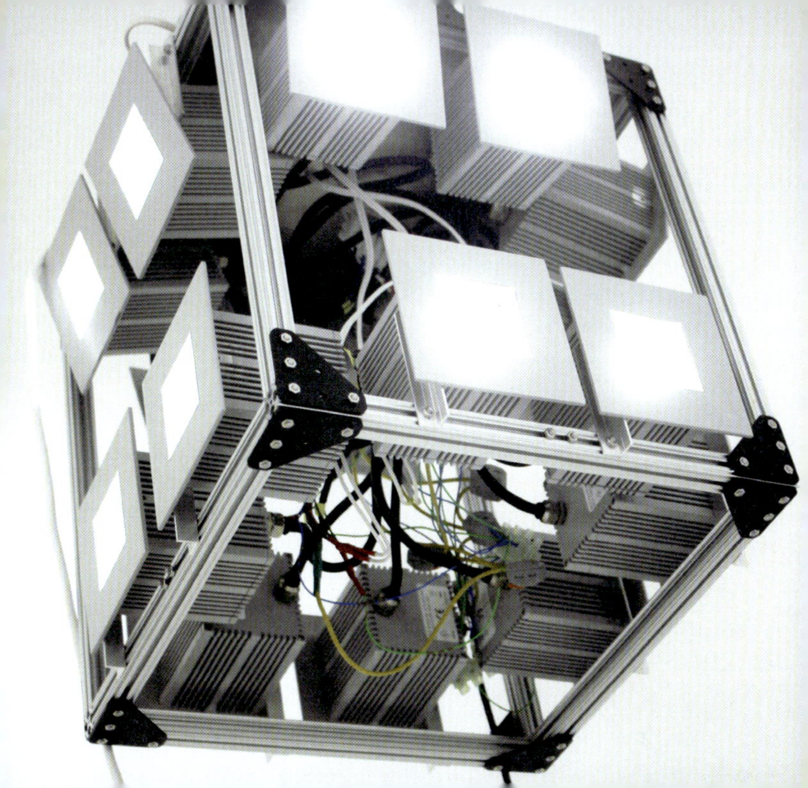

LIGHTCUBE 01

Lightcube 01 contained 16 individual spots and was suspended from the center of Room A's ceiling. Each side's four spots were directed at one exhibition wall, which were all evenly illuminated.

In Room A, a wired DMX (Digital MultipleX) system using the Loxone Smart-Home software on a PC was used to control Lightcube 01. Though each lamp of the Lightcube could be individually controlled, all were set equally during Phase 01. A slider allowed the lighting to be set anywhere within the range of 2,700 K to 6,500 K. Since the value displayed on the controls differed from the actual value (especially in the higher color-temperature ranges), spectrometer measurements were made for each light setting in the space, so that the displayed and actual values at each step were calibrated.

LIGHTCUBE 02

In Room B, Lightcube 02 also contained 16 individual spots and was suspended from the center of the ceiling. Each side's four spots were directed at one exhibition wall, which were all evenly illuminated.

Room B's illuminants were controlled wirelessly using USB Neo-Link Air and myPI-LED software installed on a PC. Though each lamp of the Lightcube could be individually controlled, all were set equally during Phase 01. The light settings could be numerically controlled in a range between 1,800 K and 16,000 K. However, in order to better compare the results from both rooms, the range actually used was limited to 2,700 K to 6,500 K. Since the value displayed on the controls differed from the actual value (especially in the higher color temperature ranges), spectrometer measurements were made for each light setting in the space, so that the displayed and actual values at each step were calibrated.

SELECTION OF ARTWORKS FOR PHASE 01

Having established a research concept for the space (Raumlabor S3T14) and having categorized artwork as either "classic/traditional," "pre-modern" and "contemporary" (resulting from analysis of the preliminary measurements, see page 119), traditional art was displayed in Room A and abstract contemporary art in Room B. The latter was a selection of three paintings from the *Spectrum 2016* series.

For Room A, I was able to draw upon the University of Applied Arts Vienna's vast archival collection of modernist artworks.

THREE PORTRAITS

The paintings from the archival collection of the University of Applied Arts Vienna, were selected together with art historian and curator Barbara Pflanzner, in consultation with the University of Vienna's Empirical Visual Aesthetics Labs. The three portraits were loaned to us for the research study 1–31 October 2017. Three portraits of women were chosen for Phase 01 of the White Cube Teleporter project (see fig. 30): a portrait of young girl by Ernst Nepo (c. 1930); a portrait of a woman by Emil Orlik (1905); and the *Portrait H. Chini* by Hans Strohofer (1921).

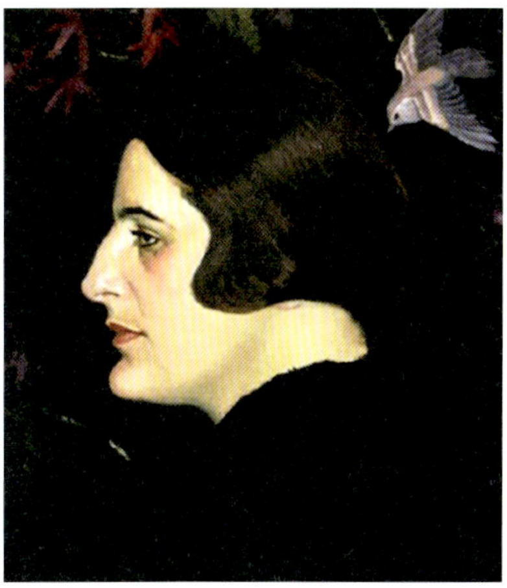

ARTWORK 01

Hans Strohofer

Portrait H. Chini, 1921

Oil on board

15.6" × 14.3"

Collection and Archive of the University of Applied Arts Vienna, inv. no. 2649/B

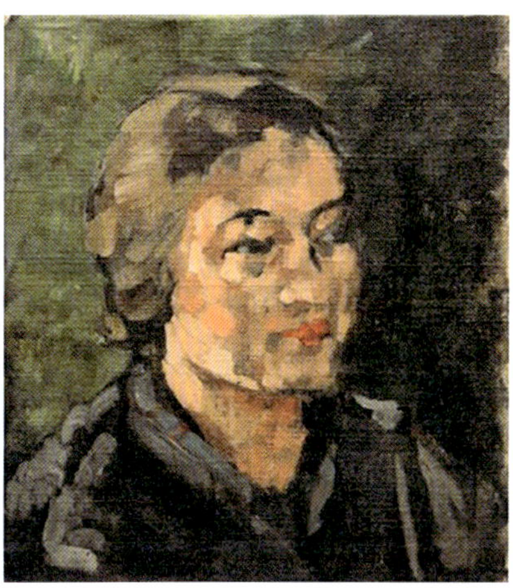

ARTWORK 02

Emil Orlik

Untitled portrait of a woman, 1905

Oil on canvas

15.6" × 14.1"

Collection and Archive of the University of Applied Arts Vienna, inv. no. 5552/B

Donation of Oswald Oberhuber

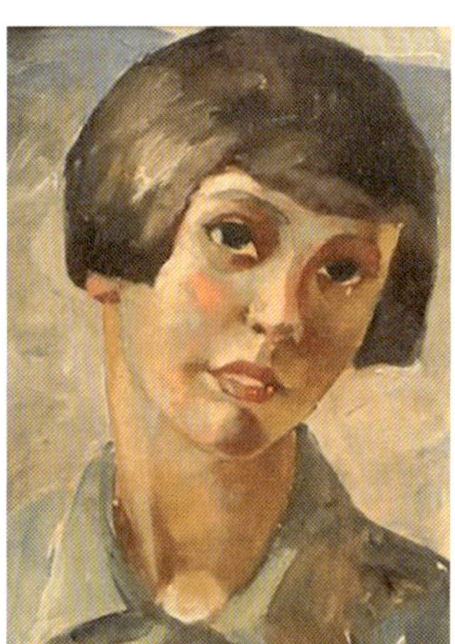

ARTWORK 03

Ernst Nepo

Untitled portrait of a young girl, c. 1930

Oil on paper

16.8" × 12.6"

Collection and Archive of the University of Applied Arts Vienna, inv. no. 4448/B

△ Figure 30. Photos of the three selected portraits

ABSTRACT ART

The artist Friedrich Biedermann's series of paintings, *Spectrum 2016*, consists of seven individual works created only a few months before the research project began. The paintings were loaned to me for use from June 2017 until January 2018. The *Spectrum 2016* series emerged from an analysis of lighting conditions; specifically, spectral measurements the artist carried out using a digital spectrometer inside selected Viennese museums and galleries. The paintings (on canvas) are composed of geometric fields of colors derived from the results of his measurements, which had been converted into RGB values and then reproduced by mixing acrylic paints. By applying different colors onto the canvas with a paint roller, the artist combined the light of the individual exhibition spaces to create his own imaginary spaces. Since the paintings' coloration is based on spectral colors, their effect can be manipulated in a controlled manner by tuning the illuminant in the research space.

For Case Study 01, three paintings from this series were selected (see fig. 31) and were pre-tested under different lighting conditions. At the conclusion of the study, all seven paintings of the *Spectrum 2016* series were exhibited under the conditions originally intended by the artist.

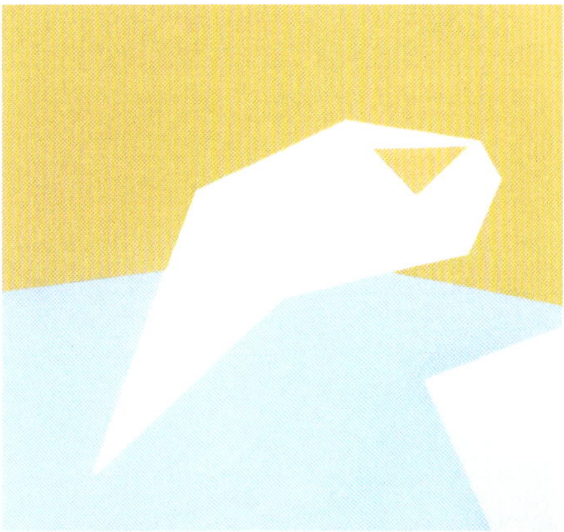

ARTWORK 04

Friedrich Biedermann
kar_mu_tho_spectrum, 2016
63" × 55"
Acrylic on canvas
On loan from the artist

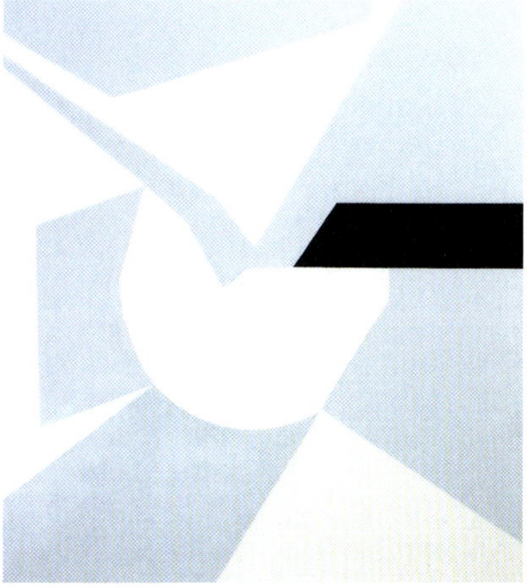

ARTWORK 05

Friedrich Biedermann
tho_alb_black_spectrum, 2016
55" × 63"
Acrylic on canvas
On loan from the artist

ARTWORK 06

Friedrich Biedermann
mu_sez_tho_spectrum, 2016
55" × 63"
Acrylic on canvas
On loan from the artist

△ Figure 31. Photos of the three abstract artworks

TRIAL RUN A

Several trial runs were carried out between July and September 2017 in preparation for Case Study 01. The three paintings selected from the series *Spectrum 2016* were tested with regard to their respective light-setting reference values. This made it possible to observe how the perception of the paintings changed under different light settings. The observations were recorded in the form of field notes and were used to determine the light settings used for Case Study 01. The trial run took place in Room B, the same space where the paintings would be displayed during the case study. Various light settings were tested, measured and preset in relation to the exhibited artworks. The paintings were centered on one of the exhibition walls in Room B and the light settings were preset according to the artist's specifications (see table 9).

TRIAL RUN A

	ARTWORK 04	ARTWORK 05	ARTWORK 06
INSTALLATION	Single painting left wall centered	Single painting middle wall centered	Single painting middle wall centered
LOCATION	Room B / S3T14	Room B / S3T14	Room B / S3T14
SKETCH OF TEST SETTING	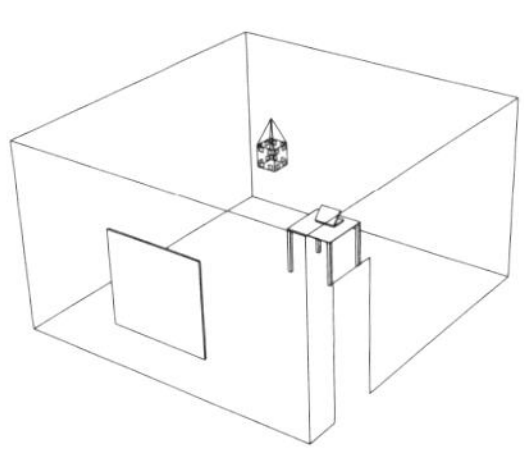	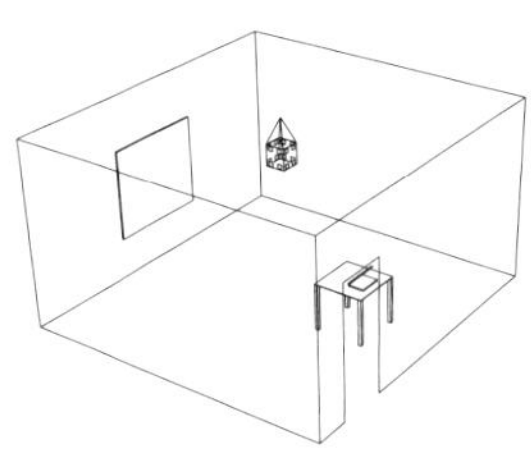	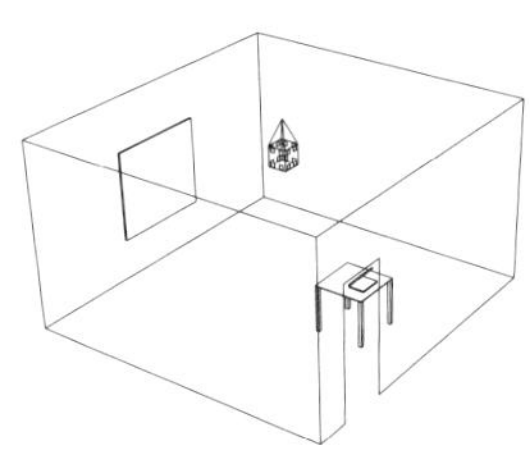
LIGHT SETTING / KELVIN	Gallery 01: 2,650 K Museum Contemporary 01: 3,572 K Gallery 02: 5,328 K	Museum Contemporary 03: 3,154 K Gallery 02: 5,328K	Museum Contemporary 01: 3,572 K Museum Contemporary 02: 4,838 K Gallery 02: 5,328 K

△ Table 9. Details on installation and light settings

TESTING AND DETERMINING THE LIGHT SETTINGS

ARTWORK 06

Artwork 06, from the *Spectrum 2016* series, is composed of three shades of color that mirror the illuminant's light color at three real exhibition spaces previously surveyed by the artist. Its composition juxtaposes color fields and color elements of differing sizes, geometrical shapes, weight and visibility. The borders are precise and the color fields do not bleed into one another.

The lighting in Room B was changed incrementally, starting with the lowest color temperature of 2,700 K and progressing through three different light settings (3,572 K / 4,838 K / 5,328 K) following Plank's curve. The images were viewed from a distance of eight feet and the following observations and impacts on visual perception were noted:

> *When the color temperature was changed rapidly, the strong contrasts of the color fields began to blur; they bled into each other. This phenomenon may be due to the fact that, as the light setting changes along Planck's curve, a dynamic interference (by gradual convergence and separation) of the three identical luminous colors in the room took place. Starting with a setting of 2,700 K, the color temperature in the room slowly and dynamically approaches the referenced lighting of Museum Contemporary 01 (3,572 K), followed by that for Museum Contemporary 02 (4,838 K), before it reaches and matches the third color temperature. The dynamism created by the changes of color temperature while viewing the painting was striking. In addition to impacting the visual perception of the artwork, it directly influenced perception of the space.*

Art and lighting merged into a complete composition. The various light settings made it possible to vividly bring out geometries and surfaces. The specific adjustment of luminous color to the real color left the impression that the displayed color matched the corresponding color temperature. The light and the specific elements of the painting became harmonized—visually unified. Neither component (light or color field) neutralized the other: Quite to the contrary, the displayed hue was enhanced by the matched lighting. The selected color field gained presence under the matching light.

ARTWORK 05

Artwork 05, from the *Spectrum 2016* series, is composed of two shades of color that mirror the color temperature of illuminants at three real exhibition spaces (measured in advance by the artist), together with the color black. The areas appear balanced, augmented by a black color field. The painting has a clear focal point around which the color fields are arranged.

Beginning with the basic setting of 2,500 K, two different light settings (3,154 K and 5,328 K) followed incrementally, which in turn represented the artist's "score"—the RAL values the artist used to mix his color palette. When viewing the artwork under various light settings, the following observations and impact on visual perception were noted:

> *The essential difference between Artwork 06 and Artwork 05 is that the latter consists of only two shades of color that would interact and be juxtaposed with each other. The emphasis shifted under the two different light settings—either one or the other color's geometric surface area would stand out. In both cases, it seemed that the emphasized color field would surround the other color field. Because the left side of the painting was dominated by the lighter color and the right side by the darker, the image dissolved toward one or the other edge of the canvas. With each light setting, this impression fluctuated. As soon as the lighting matched one of the two hues, it was perceived as being pleasant. The effect of the black color field on the overall composition seemed ambiguous to me. Despite its size and position, it seemed surprisingly neutral, receded into the background and had no impact on the surrounding color fields. It neither distracted nor irritated. Even if you kept your focus on it for a while before panning back to the other colors, there was no significant change in perception.*

ARTWORK 04

Artwork 04, from the *Spectrum 2016* series, is composed of three shades of color that mirror the luminous colors of three real exhibition spaces previously surveyed by the artist. The distribution of colors divides the composition into two halves—top and bottom are separated by an arced dividing "line." The composition is also anchored by geometric elements in the middle and in the lower right corner.

Following the artist's "score," three different light settings were tested and the following observations were noted:

> *As with the previous artwork, the light temperatures were changed incrementally from the lowest to the highest Kelvin value. At first, the color temperature was aligned with the top half of the image. Then, the bright areas in the middle and lower corner became prominent. Finally, the eye's focus shifted to the bottom half. When viewed for a longer time, the painting's foreground and background appeared to shift. The object seemed to hover in front of the two-toned background.*
>
> *The image seemed to come into its own as soon as this central geometric motif was articulated by the lighting. The background and foreground became strongly anchored allowed the painting's composition to be structured around it.*
>
> *Surprisingly, the image lost its vitality and depth effect as soon as the color temperature matched the painting's lower-half color.*

INTERPRETING THE RESULTS

In the course of viewing Artwork 06 under changing light temperatures, two different phenomena could be observed. On the one hand, lighting could be used to selectively bring out image elements (by aligning color temperature to the painting's coloration). On the other hand, the image was literally animated by dynamically altering the lighting along Planck's curve (2,700 K to 6,500 K). With a juxtaposition of only two colors, as was the case for Artwork 05, one could detect the play of contrasts. Emphasizing one of the two colors by adjusting the correlated color temperature would create a pleasant effect. In the case of Artwork 06, neither any emphasis nor any methodical rhythm could be detected. With Artwork 06, the light delineated the painting into foreground and background and appeared to animate the focal element. All tests have shown that lighting changes the perception of the viewed artwork and that aspects of the paintings' compositions can be changed dynamically depending on the lighting. The paintings form a dialogue with the lighting, which was the artist's intention.

Similar analyses were also performed on the three portraits. Photographic details of the three portraits reveal how different lighting conditions affect their coloration. The following photos (see fig. 32 and fig. 33) show stills from a two-minute time-lapse film documenting how the portraits changed under illuminants programmed to emulate the course of natural daylight. The lighting conditions changed along Planck's curve. The film clearly demonstrates the sequential changes that the changing color temperatures gave to the facial features of the women depicted in the portraits.

Since some light settings worked better than others at strengthening the color compositions of all six selected artworks, there would certainly be those that more strongly impacted the viewer's perception of them. In Case Study 01, we sought to confirm whether the lighting in the White Cube influences our appreciation of art.

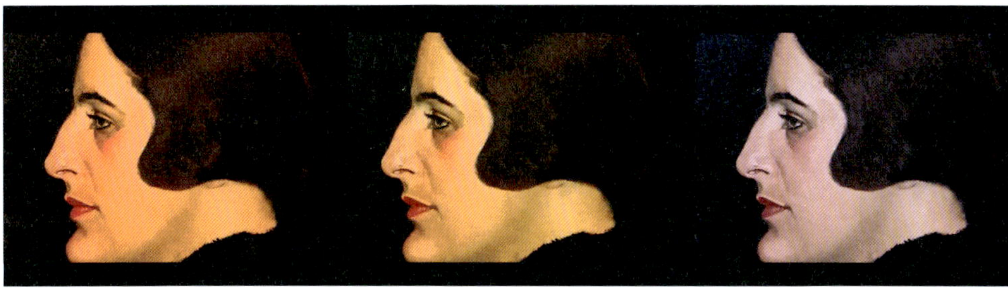

△ Figure 32. Film stills: *Portrait H. Chini* (detail), 1921, by Hans Strohofer, oil on board, Collection and Archive of the University of Applied Arts Vienna, inv. no. 2649/B

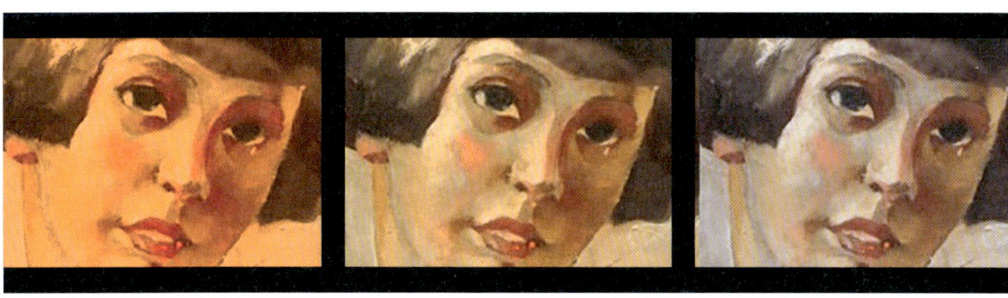

△ Figure 33. Film stills: Untitled portrait of a young girl (detail), c. 1930 by Ernst Nepo, oil on paper, Collection and Archive of the University of Applied Arts Vienna, inv. no. 4448/B

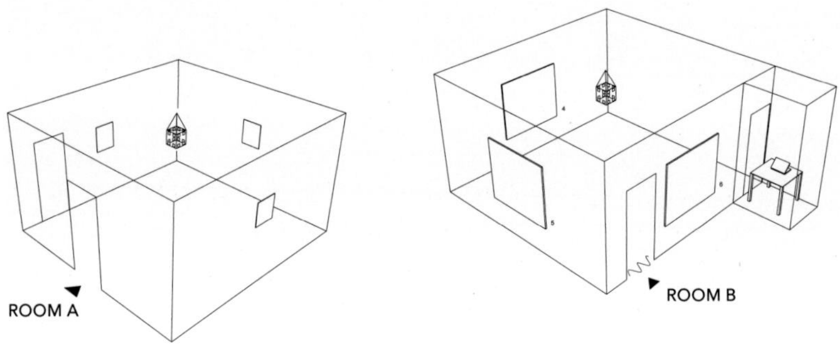

△ Figure 34. Sketch, Room A and B

CASE STUDY 01

In Case Study 01, we examined how lighting influences our spontaneous aesthetic observation of real artworks and tried to get to the bottom of the question "Does Gallery Lighting Really Have an Impact on Appreciation of Art?" (cf. Pelowski, Leder, Graser et al. 2019). The study consisted of two parts: in the first stage, the test subjects evaluated the selected artworks in both exhibition spaces (Room A and Room B) under three different light settings; in the second stage, each test subject could independently choose the light setting that was subjectively most appropriate. The test subjects were not informed that the study was about illumination of artwork. Rather, they were instructed to evaluate the art itself and to note how they felt while viewing the works.

PARTICIPANTS

For this study, 63 people (32 women and 31 men) with an average age of 23.63 participated. Many aspects determine where and how art is experienced. In addition to lighting, the art itself and the exhibition space play important roles, along with other factors, including the viewer's background and personality (cf. Pelowski et al. 2017).

EXPERIMENTAL DESIGN

Our intention was to create an experimental space that simulated an actual art gallery. For this purpose, the Raumlabor S3T14 (described in detail on pages 138–145), was launched as a temporary gallery space and equipped with a lighting system designed for this purpose. The authenticity of the rooms, despite all their *flaws* (e.g., electrical sockets, cover caps), was confirmed by the University of Vienna research team. The setups of other experimental studies proved to be more sterile and artificial in comparison to ours. According to Pelowski, there are significant differences between how art is perceived in the laboratory versus a real-world context (cf. Pelowski et al. 2017). A viewer evaluates art differently depending on whether it is displayed in a research lab or in a gallery. The use of real artwork within a research space simulating a natural environment is what differentiates our lighting study from most other comparable ones, allowing us to take a step further. It was also important for us to focus the viewer's attention on the art and not on the lighting.

PROCESS

Upon entering, the test subjects were given a questionnaire on which to record their detailed evaluation of the artwork. The questions were designed to focus their observations on the *artwork* rather than the lighting. After the study, when I asked the test subjects if they realized the research was about lighting, their replies were consistently negative. It is also worth mentioning that the subjects' appraisals were spontaneous—the artwork was new and previously unknown to them. Viewing the artwork as if in a gallery, they could enter the rooms and independently decide from which point of view and in which order they viewed the artworks, as well as how long to view each painting. The process was thus quite similar to how they would visit a real exhibition.

RESULTS AND DISCUSSION

During the trial runs leading up to the study, we were able to observe how different light settings visibly changed the selected artworks. The changes were obvious enough to us that we could reasonably assume that the lighting would also affect our test subjects' perceptions. However, it soon became apparent that the different light settings had little impact on the study results. It could not be definitively ascertained whether the respective light setting caused a painting to be perceived as more beautiful or more interesting. One explanation could be that our eyes can adapt quickly to different lighting conditions (cf. Fairchild et al. 1995). In the course of evaluating data from the study, we identified only one outlying result: the data show that the abstract art viewed under the highest color temperature tested (setting 3, at 5,328 K) was perceived negatively by the test subjects.

Nevertheless, we could observe another significant effect.

Since the study was designed to display the representational portraits and the abstract artworks in separate rooms, we could determine a correlation between the displayed art styles and the preferred color temperatures. The results showed that warm light (low color temperatures) was preferred for abstract art and cool light (high color temperatures) for the portraits. This is counterintuitive to the prevailing methods of lighting in museums, where portraits and oil paintings are usually illuminated with warm light, while contemporary or abstract art is predominantly displayed under cool light (as can be seen in the measurements taken at the reference museums, see table 7, page 119). One possible reason for this is that viewers need to apply a soft filter on abstract art. In this case, warm lighting is tantamount to soft focus. Portraiture is a more familiar and customary style to us, so apparently, we prefer to view it under cool lighting that accentuates the facial characteristics. This correlation was most evident in connection with the *Portrait H. Chini* by Hans Strohofer (see fig. 32, page 157)

The impact of lighting on viewers was generally more apparent with portraits than with abstract artwork. One can conclude that portraits are a more familiar medium to us. The viewer could definitively perceive whether the portrait's skin tone appeared orange, blue or gray. It is known that different skin tones affect our associations—for example, a person with a gray visage is perceived as sickly. Researchers at Ohio State University have found that one's facial complexion even discloses one's emotional state (cf. Benitez-Quiroz, Martinez et al. 2018: pages 3581–3586). Facial coloration can thus betray an underlying emotion that the facial expression may conceal. Such findings have been duly noted by developers of humanoid robots.

The results from the second phase, in which the test subjects could choose their own light setting (assuming the role of a curator), were surprising for their wide range of variation (2,631 K to 5,672 K). When averaged, however, the mean value of 3,776 K is close to the ideal value of 3,600 K determined by Scuello et al. (2004b). However, if the results of the previously referenced studies are analyzed individually, they reflect the diversity of findings shown by different light studies. While some studies have shown that we prefer a low color temperature for viewing art (cf., e.g., Scuello et al. 2004b), other studies demonstrate exactly the opposite and establish an ideal color temperature value in the neighborhood of 5,500 K (cf., e.g., Nascimento and Masuda 2014). Thus, experts' approaches to lighting appear to be very subjective, and the question of the best lighting for art might never be answered unequivocally. Despite this ambiguity, it goes without saying that lighting plays an essential role in museums. Of course, in addition to the choosing illumination for aesthetic concerns—to stage the artwork in the best possible lighting—conservation aspects also play an essential role (cf., e.g., Veitch and McColl 2001). Since the damage potential of the LED technology we used is negligible, this particular aspect was disregarded.

In Case Study 01, we focused on two technical dimensions: color temperature in Kelvin and illuminance in lux. Adjusting these two factors has a visible impact on the paintings' appeal, allowing their textures and coloration (among other aspects) to be brought out. Therefore, these technical variables have been the focus of several studies (see Pinto et al. 2008; Nascimento and Masuda 2014; Pridmore 2017). The selection of light settings distinguishes our study from the others. The various color temperatures in the first phase were based exclusively on reference values measured at existing museums and galleries. This means that our goal was not to compare warm color temperatures with cool ones, for example, but we rather associated the diverse light settings with different museum typologies, in order to ascertain whether their impact on artworks is evaluated differently, accordingly.

CASE STUDY 01

	LIGHT SETTING	CCT (Kelvin)	ILLUMINANCE (Lux)	CRI	MUSEUM TYPE
ROOM A (PORTRAITS)	Setting 1	3,175	580	93	Traditional
	Setting 2	3,572	590	92	Contemporary
	Setting 3	4,838	505	87	Modern Contemporary
ROOM B (ABSTRACT ART)	Setting 1	3,572	590	92	Contemporary
	Setting 2	4,838	505	87	Modern Contemporary
	Setting 3	5,328	520	86	Contemporary

△ Table 10. Light settings for the test setups in Room A and Room B

For Case Study 01, six light settings were selected according to the CCT (Correlated Color Temperature) and lux (illuminance) levels we measured at reference museums in Vienna (see tabe 10). These settings represented a cross-section of the exhibition spaces we had previously surveyed.

In each research study room, the light settings of three main museum types (traditional, contemporary and modern/contemporary) were deployed, according to the categorization we made in the course of evaluating the surveyed reference values. In our experimental design, the artworks were deliberately shown under all three different light settings, as if they were displayed in different types of museums, and thus the portraits were also shown under the light typical of contemporary art museums (contemporary).

For this study, one of three fixed light settings was used in the two rooms during each phase. Each test subject experienced only one light setting per room and was not given a choice. Perhaps the results would have been less ambiguous if the test subject had been given a second opportunity to evaluate the artwork under a different light setting. However, this would have contradicted the concept behind viewing of the images spontaneously within an experimental setup simulating a *real* exhibition experience.

Yet this would have come closer to answering the intrinsic question of my work: what is the potential of dynamic illuminants? The first study did not prove definitively that lighting makes an emotional impact on a viewer's experience of the displayed artworks. In the second phase of the study, in which the test subject could independently choose the color temperature for the exhibited artwork, quite different preferences were demonstrated. Whereas in the first experimental setup, the subjects each experienced one of the three preset light settings in one of the two rooms, now the light source was now dynamically adjustable.

Perhaps some kind of juxtaposition is required, so that we can assess what type of lighting makes art more subjectively appealing. This hypothesis significantly shaped the design of all the ensuing test setups. The deliberate staging of art became the focus of my research with the exhibition *One Artist / Two White Cubes / Five Museums*, which took place at the end of Phase 01, and became an intrinsic part of all my subsequent experiments.

TRIAL RUN B: ONE ARTIST / TWO WHITE CUBES / FIVE MUSEUMS

The exhibition *One Artist / Two White Cubes / Five Museums* was a public event at the pop-up gallery Raumlabor S3T14. The exhibition opening took place on 6 December 2017. It was well attended and the interaction between art, dynamic lighting, space and audience was distinctly noticeable. The exhibition was on view for 14 days and showcased all seven paintings from the artist Friedrich Biedermann's series, *Spectrum 2016*. It was the first time that the entire series was exhibited and the paintings' colors could interact with the lighting in the exhibition spaces of the pop-up gallery Raumlabor S3T14. One could argue that the impact of dynamic illuminants gave the paintings a new dimension.

Four of the paintings were installed in Room B, where the viewing audience was presented with the choice of five different lighting settings (see table 11). The artist had selected these settings from the actual lighting measurements of museums and galleries originally surveyed.

TRIAL RUN B – ROOM B

LIGHT SETTING	CCT (Kelvin)	MUSEUM TYPE
Setting 01	2850	Pre-modern/Modern
Setting 02	3320	Traditional
Setting 03	3830	Modern/Contemporary
Setting 04	5390	Contemporary
Setting 05	6020	Contemporary

△ Table 11. Light settings in Room B

The colors of the paintings represented the color temperatures of the light settings. To produce his canvases, the artist mixed acrylic paints to produce RGB values that corresponded to values measured in real museums and galleries. His compositions represented the light settings of the selected exhibition spaces. Due to its gray concrete flooring, Room B gave a cool and sterile impression, accentuated by the room's acoustics—every step one took reverberated audibly.

Because of this, I decided to display the four cooler paintings (those composed of higher color temperatures) in Room B.

The remaining three paintings from the *Spectrum 2016* series were displayed in Room A under dynamic lighting. All five light settings deployed in Room B were here automatically cycled; each setting lasted 12 seconds and the entire cycle repeated every minute. The transition from one setting's color temperature to another was abrupt. The illuminance was reduced by 50% for all luminaires.

TRIAL RUN B – ROOM A

LIGHT SETTING	CCT (Kelvin)	DURATION (Secs.)	MUSEUM TYPE
Setting 01	2850	12	Pre-modern/Modern
Setting 02	3320	12	Pre-modern
Setting 03	3830	12	Modern/Contemporary
Setting 04	5390	12	Contemporary
Setting 05	6020	12	Contemporary

△ Table 12. Light settings in Room A

The series of photos (see figs. 35–39) clearly shows just how differently the series of paintings appeared under the dynamic lighting. The photos show Room A under the five light settings, which were automatically switched dynamically, as described above.

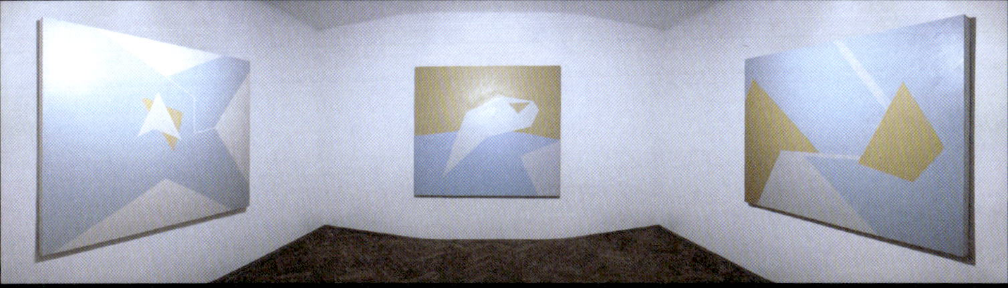
△ Figure 35. Light setting Museum 01, Raumlabor S3T14

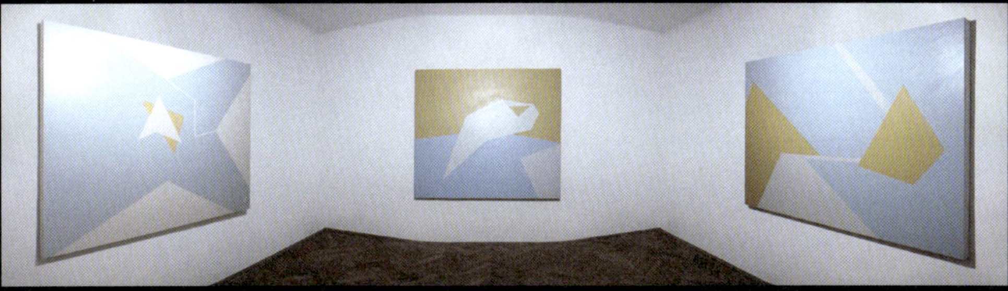
△ Figure 36. Light setting Museum 02, Raumlabor S3T14

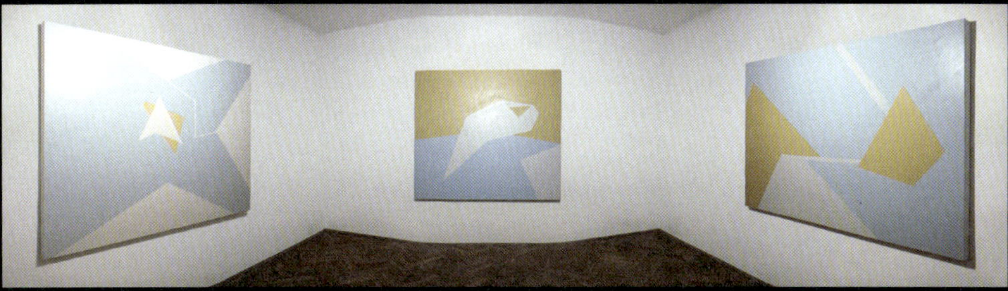
△ Figure 37. Light setting Museum 03, Raumlabor S3T14

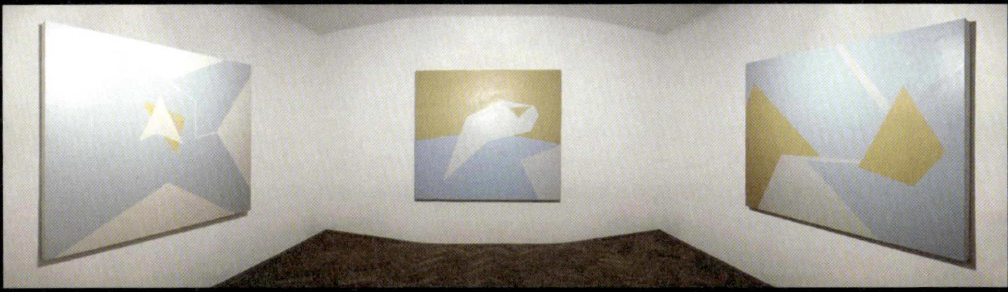
△ Figure 38. Light setting Museum 04, Raumlabor S3T14

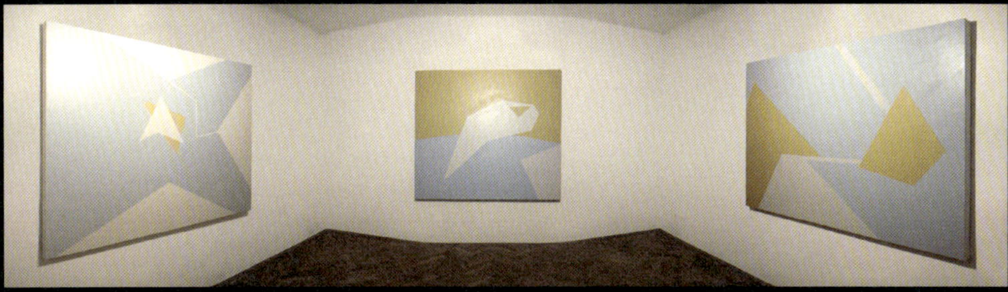
△ Figure 39. Light setting Museum 05, Raumlabor S3T14

A diverse audience attended the opening event. At the time, most of them were unfamiliar with the topic of museum lighting. But soon, lively discussions were taking place about lighting's role in the perception of art. Differing preferences were declared, reaffirming my view that the perception of lighting can be quite subjective. With few exceptions, the cycling of dynamic light settings every 12 seconds was received quite positively and encouraged the attendees to linger.

This test setup made it clear that artificial lighting can interact with the artwork. The expressive strength of the paintings changed significantly depending upon the light setting. In Room B, most visitors preferred the light setting with the highest color temperature of 6,020 K. This is quite interesting, given that most museums and galleries favor much lower color temperatures.

By the end of the exhibition, I was assured that customizing the illuminants to harmonize with the artwork seemed worthwhile. It was only through the changes in light settings that the diversity of the images became evident and lighting emerged as a variable and protagonist. The potential of dynamic lighting also became apparent. The presentation of art in a museum makes certain assumptions about how a visitor will prefer viewing it. Installing art is the domain of the exhibition designers, the curators and the artists. By deploying dynamic illuminants, museums can give the viewing public an interactive role in the exhibition.

PHASE 02—
CASE STUDY 02: FIVE ARTISTS × FIVE MUSEUMS

During Phase 02, Case Study 02 took place in the form of a public exhibition on view 4–24 October 2018. Carrying out the research project in an actual exhibition context presented me with new challenges. The exhibition space in the Angewandte Interdisciplinary Lab (AIL) met all requirements for a White Cube experiment, and so this large room in the basement became the testing space for the White Cube Teleporter project during both Phase 02 and Phase 03. The Lightcubes (described on pages 142–145) were adapted to the new requirements of an actual exhibition gallery and its spatial proportions, so that a uniform illumination of the exhibition walls was achieved.

The exhibition was titled *Five Artists × Five Museums*. The idea was to exhibit five artworks by five contemporary artists under five light settings that reproduced at AIL the lighting measured at existing White Cubes.

The light settings could be dialed up either manually or dynamically, enabling the creation of an interactive lighting laboratory for art and architecture, thus positioning digitized light as a potential artistic tool. Within this environment, an immediate interaction of light, space and art was created. Once again, the question was how we, as designers and artists, can conceive and make full use of digital-lighting tools.

RESEARCH SPACE—EXHIBITION SPACE AIL, BASEMENT

The rectangular exhibition room in the basement of the AIL met the definition of a classic White Cube: white walls and ceiling; gray floor; and artificially illuminated. The exhibition space measured about 970 square feet (~56' × 17.5'). The ceiling was nearly 15 feet high, allowing the illuminants to be installed above the level of the artworks. The large-scale artwork *Cells of Hypersphere* was the only piece on which the illuminants' reflection was visible, yet only unobtrusively in its uppermost area.

With its white walls and concrete floor, the room gave a coldish impression. Ambient noise from the floor above was audible here below. The walls were painted white with Brillux Super Latex elf 3000. The room's existing luminaires (fluorescent tube lamps) were completely turned off for the duration of the exhibition. The natural light from the overhead window recesses was blocked out and the room's sole light source were the Lightcubes.

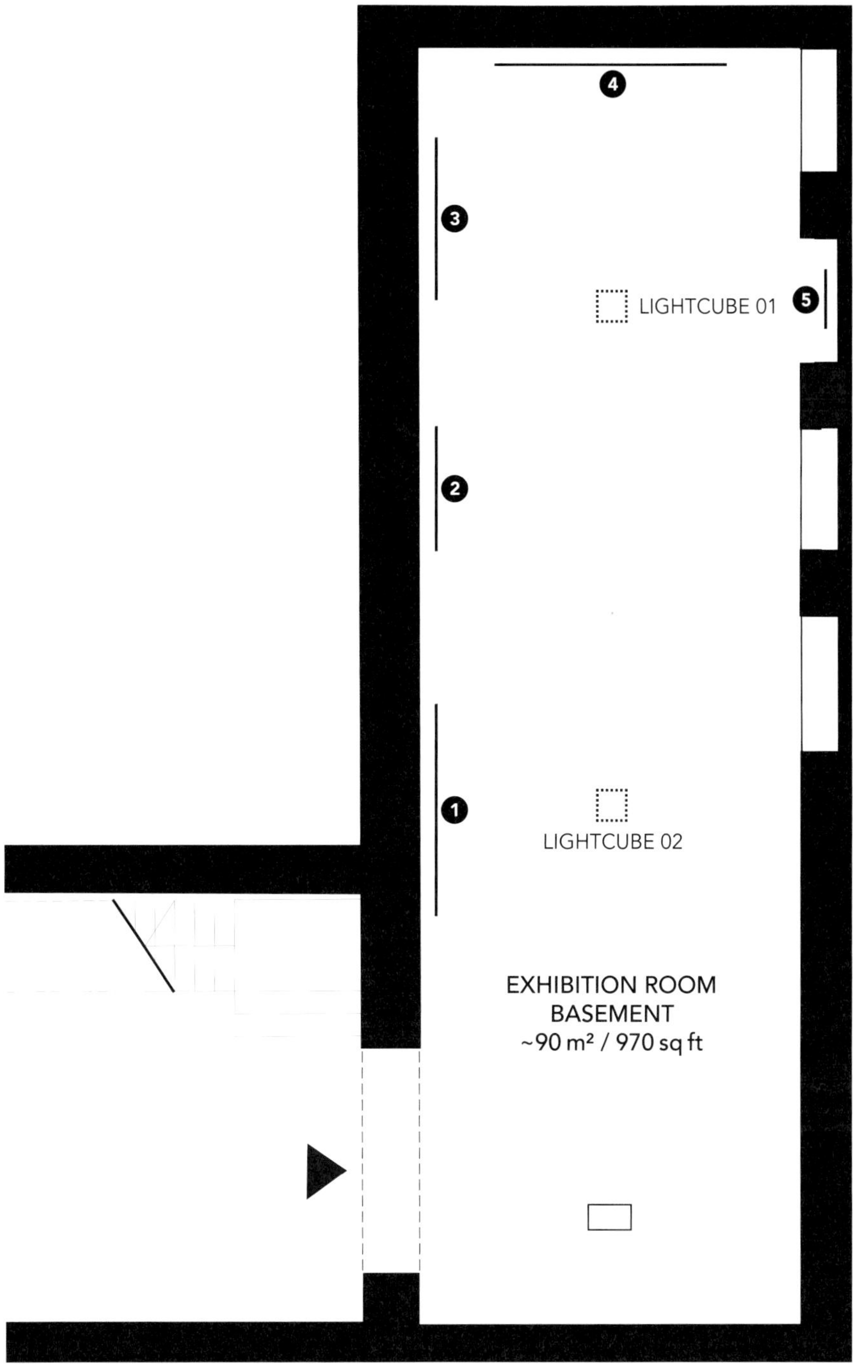

1. Gregor Eldarb, *Redite (Version N°3)*, 2016/17
2. Friedrich Biedermann, *kar_mu_tho spectrum*, 2016
3. Bernd Oppl, *Black Rooms*, 2017–2020
4. Alina Kunitsyna, *Cells of Hyperspheres*, 2015
5. Fauke Dannert, *Dolde*, 2016

△ Figure 40. Floor plan of AIL White Cube, Case Study 02, *Five* × *Five* exhibition

ARTIFICIAL LIGHTING

Five artworks were displayed under five different light settings. The light settings were based on lighting measurements previously taken at actual exhibition spaces. Here, the lighting changed dynamically; partly automatically, partly on demand at the push of a button. To this end, the Phase 01 Lightcubes were adapted to spatial and functional requirements.

CASE STUDY 02: LIGHTCUBE 01 & 02

LIGHT SETTING	LUX	CCT (Kelvin)	MUSEUM TYPE
M1 / SECESSION	150	5,000	Contemporary
M2 / MUMOK	150	3,500	Modern/Contemporary
M3 / KHM	150	2,700	Traditional
M4 / BELVEDERE 21	150	4,100	Contemporary
M5 / MAK	150	2,900	Contemporary

△ Table 13. Light settings for Lightcube 01 & 02

The illuminance of 150 lux represented the averaged value of the museums surveyed.

LIGHTCUBE 01

PiLED Client software enabled Lightcube 01 to be controlled wirelessly. It executed a pre-programmed, dynamic lighting sequence modeled on the light settings measured at five museums. The intensity was set to 100-percent brightness. Each light setting lasted 20 seconds before automatically changing to the next preset. The entire sequence repeated every 100 seconds. Six of the Lightcube's individual spots were aimed at the side wall, four aimed at the front wall, and another four aimed toward the wall recess.

LIGHTCUBE 02

The Lightcube 02 in the front half of the room consisted of 16 spots that were controlled (as a single unit) by a wired DMX (Digital MultipleX) system employing Loxone Smart-Home software. Twelve of the 16 spots were directed at the front wall, evenly illuminating the artwork *Redite (Version N°3)* by Gregor Eldarb. The Lightcube was suspended from the ceiling and its bottom panel was 9 feet (2.8 m) above the floor. Using a tablet device, an exhibition viewer could select any one of the following five museum-lighting presets (the transitions were immediate and abrupt).

ARTWORK

The selection of artwork was facilitated by the artists' enthusiasm to support the research project. The works on display by the five artists—Friedrich Biedermann, Frauke Dannert, Gregor Eldarb, Alina Kunitsyna and Bernd Oppl—shared an emphasis on spatial themes. Subjective interpretations of space, spatial collages and hypothetical spatial constructions formed a dialogue and, taken together, they invited the beholder to explore a new way to experience visual space. The artificial lighting of the exhibition space became the unifying element. An overview of the artworks on display can be seen in figures 41–45. Here, in contrast to Phase 01, an investigation of the White Cube as a functional exhibition space and the survey of the illuminants played secondary roles. In this phase, the focus was rather on exploring how lighting could be an active participant in a dialogue between the art, the viewer and the space.

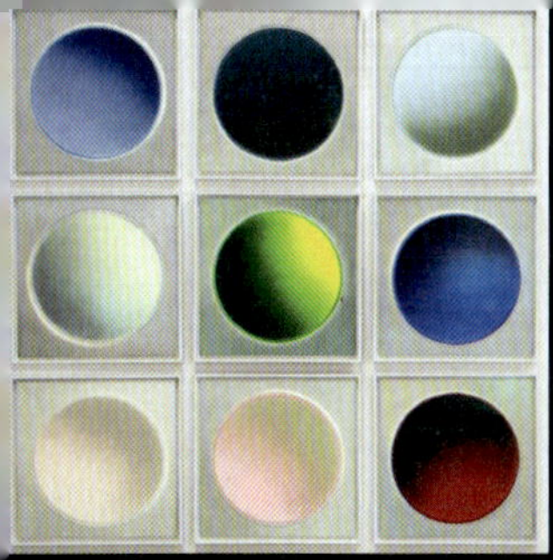

◁ Figure 41. Alina Kunitsyna, *Cells of Hypersphere*, 2015, ink on paper plus frames, 9 pieces, 27.5" × 27.5"

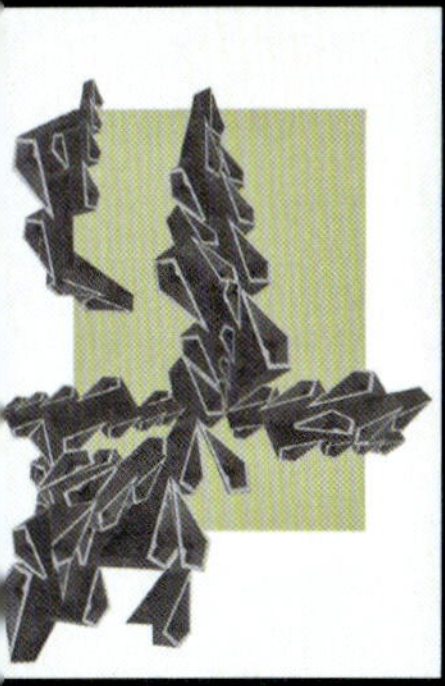

◁ Figure 42. Frauke Dannert, *Dolde*, 2016, paper collage, 18.5" × 13"

▽ Figure 43. Bernd Oppl, *Black Rooms*, 2017–2020, photo print, 5 pieces, 16.5" × 11.7"

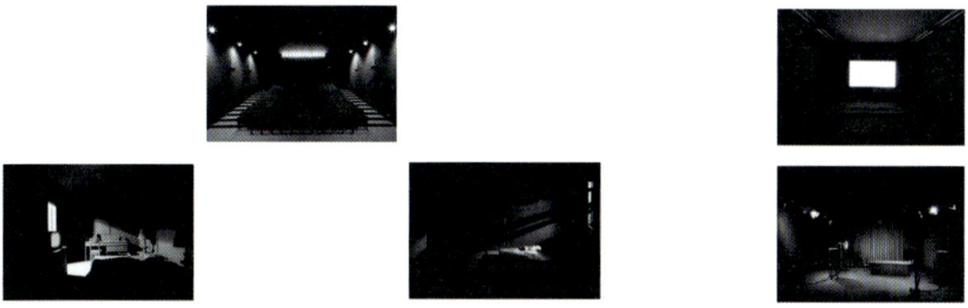

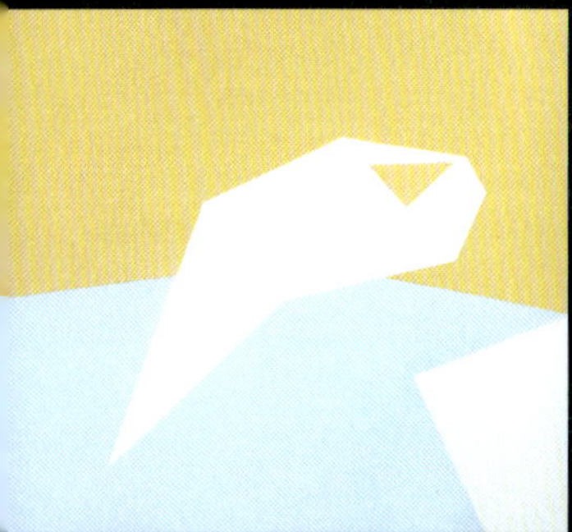

◁ Figure 44. Friedrich Biedermann, *kar_mu_tho spectrum*, 2016, acrylic on canvas, 55" × 63"

▽ Figure 45. Gregor Eldarb, *Redite (Version N°3)*, 2016–2017, series of 22 small-format collages; inkjet, oil, acrylic, pastel on linen bookcloth / cardboard

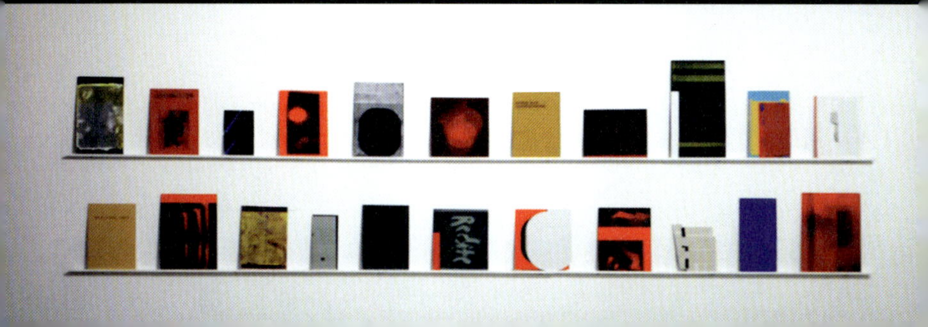

TEST PROCESS / METHODS OF IMPLEMENTATION

Case Study 02 took place as a public exhibition. The viewing audience was part of the experiment. The opening event was attended by artists, curators, art historians, art students, journalists, architects, doctors, perceptual psychologists and publishers, among others. Some of the recipients were already familiar with the artworks, yet they entered the experiment without any preconceived notions, as visitors to an art exhibition. The artwork was installed without any predetermined viewing sequence; the public could independently choose which artwork to view first and in which order to proceed. In this way, attendees could find their own preferred point of entry and the experience was very similar to a real art gallery visit.

It became clear that their preferences were quite disparate. It would happen, that if a visitor would take an interest in the art of Bernd Oppl, for example, first she would focus her attention exclusively on the artwork and then gradually observe it under dynamic light settings. Someone else would begin by viewing Gregor Eldarb's artwork, which was illuminated exclusively by Lightcube 02. Here, the viewer could manually select from among five different light settings, which were designated on the tablet's display according to the museum each setting simulated. Knowing the source had an apparent effect on how the audience engaged with the experiment. Often, an attendee would recall a previous visit to one of these museums, thus building some associations between past and present.

The five light settings could be changed by tapping an option on the tablet's touchscreen. It could be recorded how often and quickly each viewer changed the lighting selection, and this varied considerably. Some people would prefer to linger under one light setting, while others would switch them quickly to get through the entire cycle. Some would choose in the order as listed from top to bottom (Museums 1 to 5), while others would compare only two specific museums. We deliberately decided not to interfere with or prompt their decision making, so that we could observe their intuitive application of the exhibition lighting.

In the rear part of the room, Lightcube 01 was programmed to automatically change the lighting mood every 20 seconds. It illuminated the artworks of Frauke Dannert, Alina Kunitsyna and Bernd Oppl. Friedrich Biedermann's painting was hung in between the two Lightcubes, illuminated by both. The light settings were set independently for each Lightcube, yet they could be deliberately synced up (see figs. 46–48).

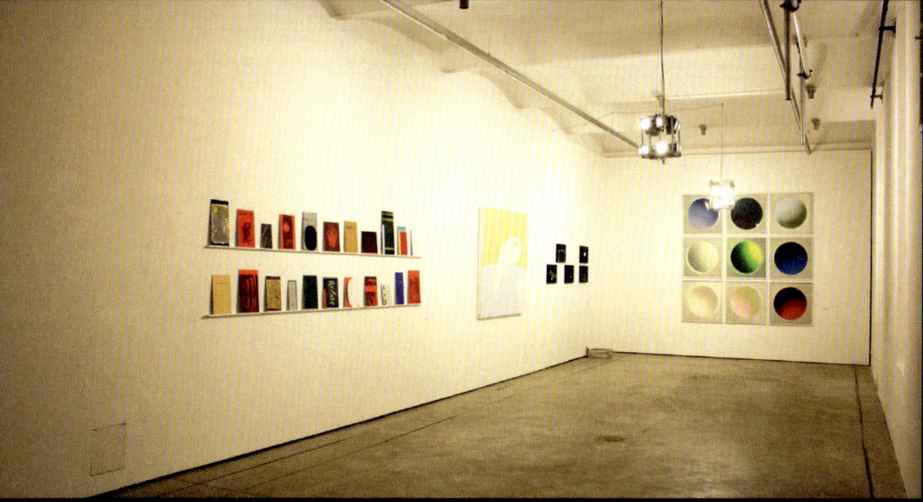

△ Figure 46. Exhibition *5 × 5* in AIL, light setting M3 for both Lightcubes (2,700 K)

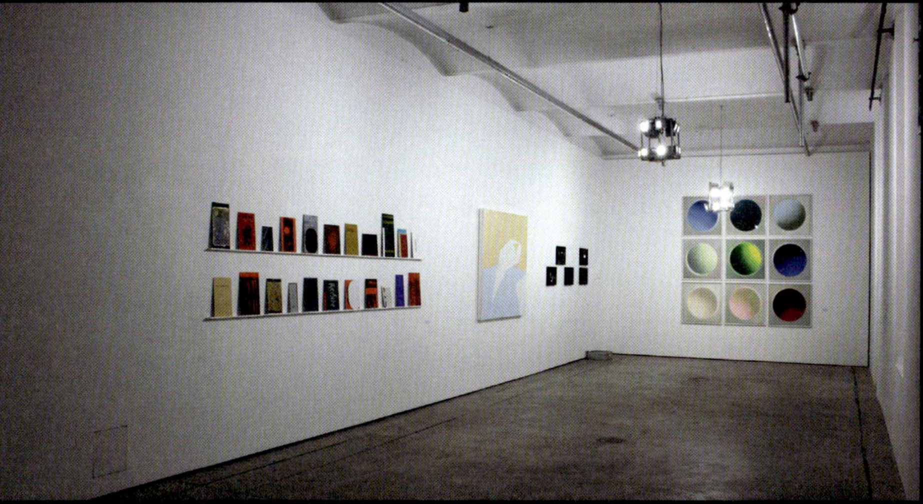

△ Figure 47. Exhibition *5 × 5* in AIL, light setting M1 for both Lightcubes (5,000 K)

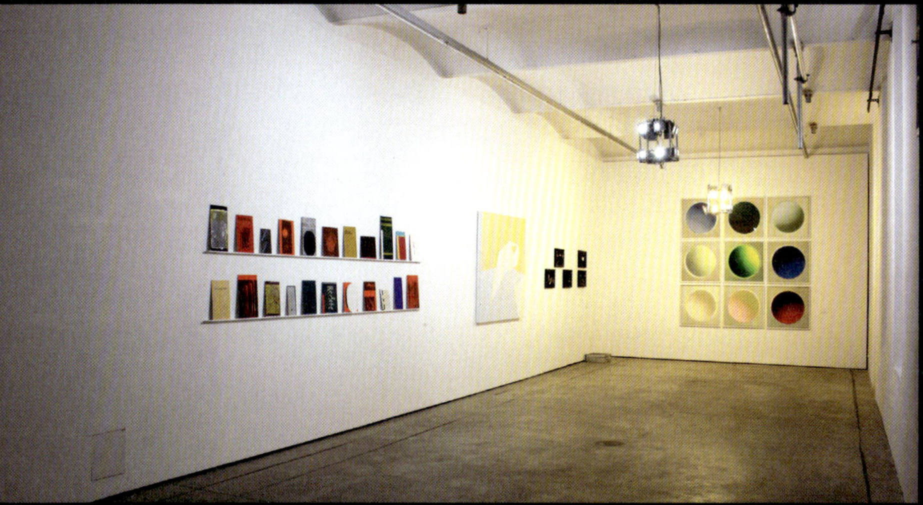

△ Figure 48. Exhibition *5 × 5* in AIL, light setting M3 for Lightcube 01 (2,700 K) and light setting M1 for Lightcube 02 (5,000 K)

OUTCOMES AND INSIGHT

The artist Gregor Eldarb (b. 1971) attended the opening event and some of the visitors came specifically to see his 2016 artwork, *Redite (Version N°3)*. As the concept behind this work requires the viewer to *read*, its legibility depended upon the generated lighting moods. The series of 22 small-format collages on linen bookcloth were displayed on two parallel, horizontal wood moldings. The collages resembled book covers aligned on two shelves, which led visitors to view them from left to right, at first. However, *Redite* is conceived to allow viewers to scan the artwork, and this was the viewing method most impacted by the experiment's light setting changes. The lighting acted as a filter and intermediary. Especially with the multilayered, red graphics of *Redite*, particularly striking changes in appearance could be observed under the different lighting moods. The lighting brought out the collages' different layers and each individual panel became animated. The artwork offered the viewer several points of entry in terms of its readability. One could view the work as a holistic image on the wall or as individual collages forming a linear series of texts. This subjective choice for approaching the art was bolstered by the ability to choose a light setting for the space. Visitors were now able to personalize their approaches to the art and the space, where normally they would be guided by the artist's and the exhibition designer's preconceived assumptions as to what is most suitable. The duration of each light setting (Lightcube 02) and the viewing of the artwork was determined solely by the person selecting the light settings.

Unlike with Lightcube 02, the viewers were not given any indication about which light setting was automatically selected for Lightcube 01, so the audience responded to the changing settings more intuitively. Their focus was mainly on the artwork. The matter of how one's visual perception of the artwork can be impacted by changes of lighting became evident only gradually.

The artwork *kar_mu_tho spectrum* (2016) by Friedrich Biedermann (b. 1975) was displayed at the center of the longer wall and was illuminated by three spots from both Lightcubes. This painting, from the series *Spectrum 2016*, was selected by the artist specifically because its high-contrast composition aptly fit to this exhibition's lighting setup. The decision to hang the painting exactly where the illumination from the two Lightcubes intersected turned out to be quite intriguing. Because the painting's color scheme was made up of luminous colors, the lighting fostered an interplay between the painted surfaces and the room. Both Lightcubes impacted our visual perception of the artwork. Unlike it was for the Phase 01 trial runs, the Lightcube was not set to match the luminous values of any of the painting's three colors, however the deviations were within a negligible range. The light settings M1 (5,000 K), M2 (3,500 K) and M3 (2,700 K) corresponded to the color scheme of the artwork, as the artist intended. The compositional hierarchy of the image changed for each viewer, depending on the light setting. By being able to adjust the settings independently, the viewer entered into an active dialogue with the artwork instead of merely assuming the role of a passive observer.

There was a two-step process in observing the painting. First, one viewed it under the automatically changing light settings of Lightcube 01; each respective light setting changed the visual impact of the color fields and the image's compositional emphasis. In the second step, the viewer was prompted to use the tablet to adjust the lighting from Lightcube 02 to augment the dynamic lighting from Lightcube 01. Each person determined his or her preferred lighting for viewing the artwork—blending the two light settings as they wished, although (unlike for *Rendite*) the illumination from Lightcube 01 was still being automatically controlled.

Most viewers preferred both the M1 and M3 light settings. That these settings represented the highest and lowest CCT values, respectively, their preference might have resulted from the more evident contrasts in the image. Yet the color temperatures of these light settings correlated to those of the lighting moods referenced by the artist, and the visual impact of the color fields became stronger under these settings.

The artwork *Black Rooms* (2017–2020) by Bernd Oppl (b. 1980) consists of black-and-white photographs of model rooms. Oppl's works deal with physical and *media* spaces and the perceptual sequences that they produce. He employs videos, photography, room models and sound. The overlapping of one medium with another creates conflict and abstraction that, in turn, provokes the viewer into developing new associations. Such was the case with *Black Rooms*, the work exhibited here. Only on closer inspection did one perceive that the depicted rooms were scale models. The content of the photos is largely revealed by a theatrical staging of light.

Black Rooms was illuminated exclusively by Lightcube 01, whose automated cycle of five light settings formed a dialogue with the lighting staged in the photos. The content of the image formed an interactive narrative between space, light and the viewer. The rooms depicted in the photos are dramatically illuminated by natural and artificial light sources. Side light and artificial lighting from above, as well as the picture's central white area resembling a movie screen, took on the leading role. By changing the light settings in the exhibition space, the lighting moods depicted in the images also changed.

This is how the images' side lighting appeared to change under the exhibition's five different light settings (color temperatures ranging from 2,700 to 5,000 K): The light shown in the photograph under the Museum 03 setting (2,700 K) corresponded to natural light in the morning/evening; under the Museum 05 setting (5,000 K—measured at midday at a museum illuminated by natural light) corresponded to daylight at midday. In one of the photos—which several visitors compared with spatial installations by the artist James Turrell—a large white surface is depicted to appear as a window. This work reminded me of Turrell's room installation, *Wide Out*, which had been exhibited at Vienna's Museum of Applied Arts (exhibition: *James Turrell, The Other Horizon,* 2 December 1998–21 March 1999). That installation blurred the boundaries of the exhibition space by using lighting to create an illusion of a rectangular, sharp-edged wall surface.

The changing lighting at the AIL exhibition space altered the color of the rectangular bright surface in Bernd Oppl's photographic work, leading the viewers to focus on this particular compositional element. As with James Turrell's spaces, the precisely directed sharp border of the light area (seamless, in James Turrell's designed space) made this surface appear as a foreground element. In the photograph, however, the bright surface appeared to recede into the background. The lighting shown in this series of photographs became animated under the exhibition lighting. The visual perception of space in these artworks was redefined over the course of Lightcube 01's 100-second cycle. The experiences gained from this test series contributed significantly to the design of Case Study 03.

Displayed on the back wall of the gallery space, *Cells of Hypersphere* (2015) by Alina Kunitsyna (b. 1981) was the first artwork one noticed upon entering the room, so it was the starting point for most visitors. *Cells of Hypersphere*, consisting of nine individually framed pictures arranged as a complete work of art, entered into a dialogue with the lighting in the space. Viewers in the exhibition space took in its subtle color play of visually perceived patterns. The bold colors of the individual images, as well as the illusion of depth created by their gradients, changed according to the lighting mood, enabling the viewer to grasp issues of lighting directly. The interaction between the nine-image artwork with the space and the lighting became visually perceptible. The works were framed behind glass, causing some lighting to be reflected in the uppermost region. The nonreflective glass used, however, minimized any distraction. The graphic appearance of each individual painting's circle/disk changed drastically over the course of the dynamic lighting sequence. The hierarchy of the artwork—which circles came forward or receded into the background—was significantly impacted by the lighting. The relationship of the individual circles to their respective backgrounds also became an issue. This interplay between lighting and artwork was observable up close and from a distance.

The work of the artist Frauke Dannert (b. 1979), *Dolde*, was discovered by the visitors only when they arrived at the rear area of the gallery, as this artwork was displayed in a recessed wall niche. This gave the rather small work a space to come into its own. The interplay of lighting with its intricate collage technique gave the viewer new perspectives on the work. The background of this collage work was white and its green color field took on different characteristics as the dynamic lighting sequence progressed.

SYNOPSIS

The exhibition *Five Artists × Five Museums* offered insights into the potentials for the dynamic illumination of exhibition spaces. The five artworks yielded quite diverse results. It appears that dynamic artificial lighting is also capable of dynamically changing our perception of a work of art. This was especially apparent with the artwork *Cells of Hypersphere*. Looking at Bernd Oppl's photo series, we also observed that lighting can impact how the subject of the image is perceived. Furthermore, the influence of lighting on the composition of the image became evident when viewing the series *Spectrum 2016* and the artwork *Redite*. Especially with the latter, one could notice that the changes in lighting mood impacted how we perceive the disposition of its individual collages.

Lighting is not only an intermediary between art and the viewer, but it also significantly affects the way we interpret and perceive art. It thus takes on a substantial role and gives the work of art a new voice, if the observer is willing to *listen*. In my opinion, however, this voice should not be homogenous, as this study demonstrated how subjectively people approach and deal with lighting. The deployment of dynamic illuminants interposes a versatile intermediary through which we view art. The experiences show that through this versatility we can create new perspectives and open up new approaches to art.

The ability to change the exhibition lighting in real time opened up new ways of viewing art. Although this experiment allowed the audience to become actively involved in setting the lighting moods, it was not intended to determine which light setting is preferred for any specific artwork. Rather, it explored the potential shown by dynamically lighting an exhibition space when viewers are allowed to perceive five different artworks under five different light settings in real time. Compared to previous studies, ours found no preference for any one of the five light settings. However, it was demonstrated that the public were discovering lighting as a medium in its own right—a medium that, when we engage with it, can change our perspectives on art and open up a new way of communicating with it.

PHASE 03— CASE STUDY 03: LIGHTHOUSE, AIL

The *Lighthouse* experiment was designed on the assumption that artificial light sources in the museum of the future will no longer be static, but dynamic and changeable. The experimental setup was co-conceived with the artist Friedrich Biedermann and took place in the form of a public exhibition at Vienna's Angewandte Interdisciplinary Lab (AIL), 20 March to 3 April 2019. Our hypothesis was that lighting essentially shapes our perception of art and space, is available to us as a design element in the White Cube and creates an interplay between art, space and light.

EXPERIMENTAL SETUP

Case Study 03 again took place in the 970-square-foot exhibition space in the basement of the AIL (Angewandte Interdisciplinary Lab) in Vienna. The room's existing lighting was completely turned off. Instead, the room, the walls and the sculpture were illuminated exclusively by the two Lightcubes. Images of the reference museums' light spectrometer readings (see, for example, figs. 20–23) were projected onto the wall to the right of the entrance, in order to inform the viewer. The sculpture *Lighthouse* was suspended from the ceiling in the rear of the room, 39 inches above the floor. The longitudinal and rear walls of the exhibition space were painted in a black-and-white geometrical pattern. To accomplish this, we projected a customized, computer-generated black-and-white image onto the white exhibition walls on and painted over the black fields with blackboard paint.

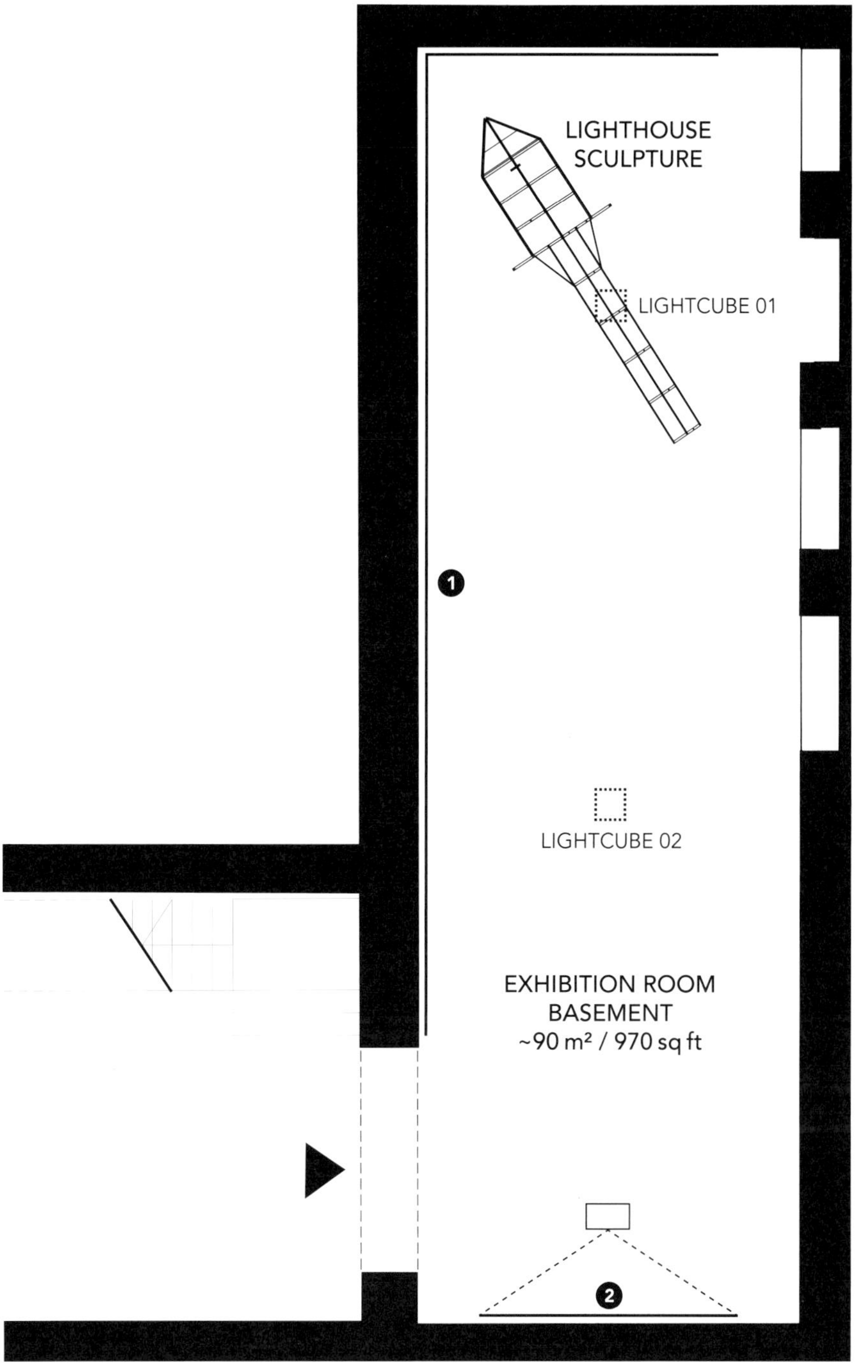

1 Wall design
2 Spectral images projection

△ Figure 49. Floorplan AIL, Case Study 03, for *Lighthouse* exhibition

LIGHTING

We installed Lightcubes 01 and 02 in the same positions as we did for Case Study 02. For this purpose, they were suspended from the ceiling with steel cables and their sides were aligned parallel to the exhibition walls. Both Lightcubes were now retrofitted to be controlled wirelessly via a tablet computer with a Neolink USB stick and the PiLED Client software. The system could now manipulate each individual illuminant of both Lightcubes, making it possible to dial up and play the pre-programmed lighting sequence simultaneously on both units. In contrast to Case Study 02, the exhibition space could now be bathed in uniform dynamic lighting.

SCULPTURE AND EXHIBITION DESIGN

Together as artist and architect, we designed the experimental set-up. The artist installed his sculpture, *Lighthouse*—a light sculpture that itself radiated dynamic lighting that simulated the chronological sequence of natural daylight, thus presenting all facets of such light. At the same time, the lighting in the exhibition space changed dynamically in the form of a lighting "script" modeled on the measurement results of 13 surveyed museums.

As an architect, I was in charge of designing the exhibition space and its walls, as well as writing the script for the museum-lighting theme. While the concept of our first experiment required purely white walls, this time we designed the walls with graphical elements (described above and below) that supported the visual perception of light. My aim was to create a new spatial experience and a new exhibition concept, using lighting as a dynamic design tool to mediate between art, space and viewer. In addition to observing the dynamic light simulation of the lighting levels measured at 13 surveyed museums, visitors saw information about which museum's lighting had just been simulated and how its respective spectral image appeared. These data were projected by beamer onto the gallery wall opposite the sculpture, allowing the audience to comprehend the connection between the active light setting, its spectrum and which original exhibition space it emulated, thus contextualizing how the artwork was being illuminated, in real time.

GRAPHIC DESIGN OF WALLS

The graphic design of the gallery walls was chosen to harmonize with the sculpture and the dynamic-lighting script. The experience gained from our previous experiments served as a point of departure.

The reflectance factor of the white wall paint (~ 90%) was contrasted with the reflectance of the matte blackboard paint (~ 4%). As the black fields absorbed the light, the white surfaces became thoroughly accentuated. The black-and-white wall graphics therefore divided the space into visible and invisible areas. The contrast intensified the viewers' focus on the white wall surfaces, whose appearance underwent constant change due to the dynamic lighting from the Lightcubes. As a result, even the smallest nuances of lighting changes could be perceived.

The application of the achromatic colors, black and white (cf. Küppers 1981: 75ff.)—which have been attributed with the character of border markings (cf. Haarmann 2005: 41)—for our experiment enhanced the perception of dynamic lighting in the gallery space. Due to their contrast with the black wall surfaces, the white ones raised the audience's awareness of the changing color of the lighting—the result of changes in color temperatures. The light, itself, became a dynamic image displayed on the exhibition walls. By displaying the light on the walls and having its reflectance pervading the space and its occupants, the lighting clearly functioned as a linchpin in the pattern of relationships we created for this experiment.

The graphic design of the exhibition space optically enveloped the sculpture on display, reinforcing its centrality and focusing the audience's attention on it (see fig. 50). The goal was to have the wall graphics create a nested space *within* the gallery's walls, turning it into a walk-in installation, allowing the audience to perceive it as an illuminated space and fully engaging them in this spatial experience.

The exhibition space was transformed by dynamic lighting, which was modeled on lighting measured at the referenced museums. Within three minutes and 33 seconds, 13 different lighting moods of 13 existing exhibition spaces illuminated the sculpture and were beheld by the audience. The goal of projecting the name and light-spectrum data of each respective museum onto the back wall simultaneously with the light setting (see fig. 51) was to activate the collective memory of the art-savvy audience and to enjoin their present experience to those they had already had in those other spaces.

The projected images displayed the spectral composition of the referenced museums' lighting, giving the audience a context to understand the variety of lighting under which we view art.

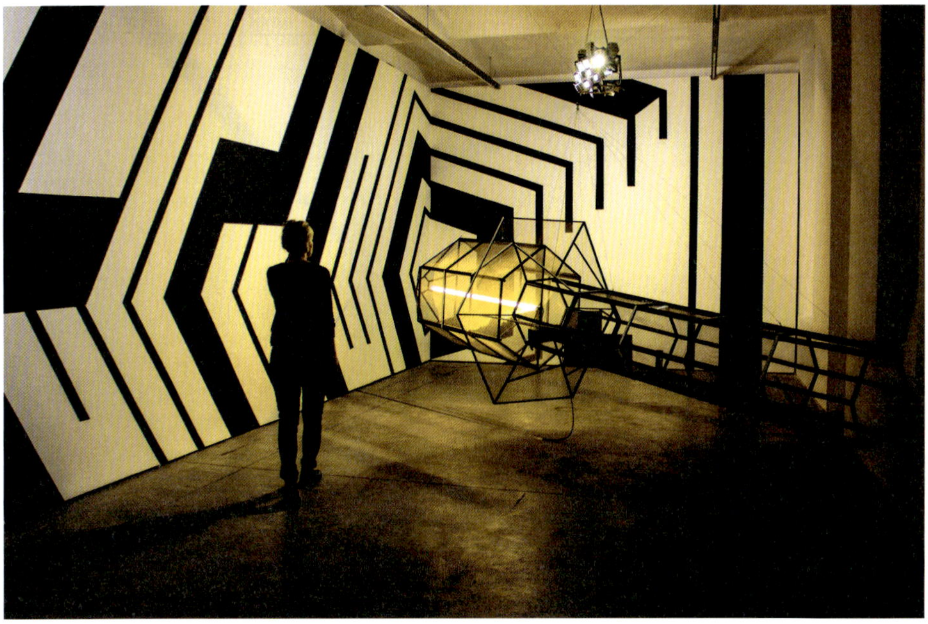

△ Figure 50. View of the *Lighthouse* exhibition space

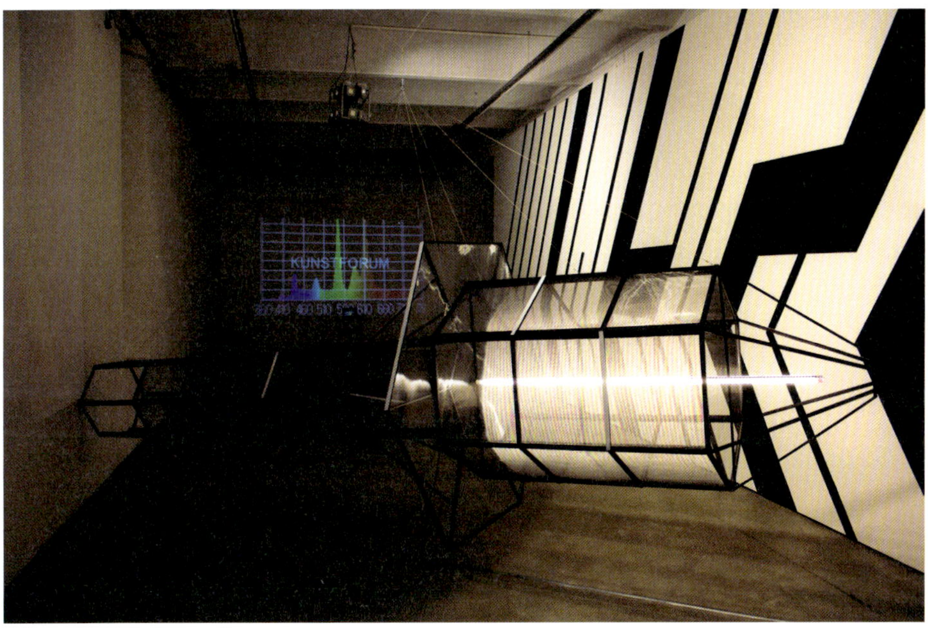

△ Figure 51. View of the *Lighthouse* exhibition space with spectral image in background

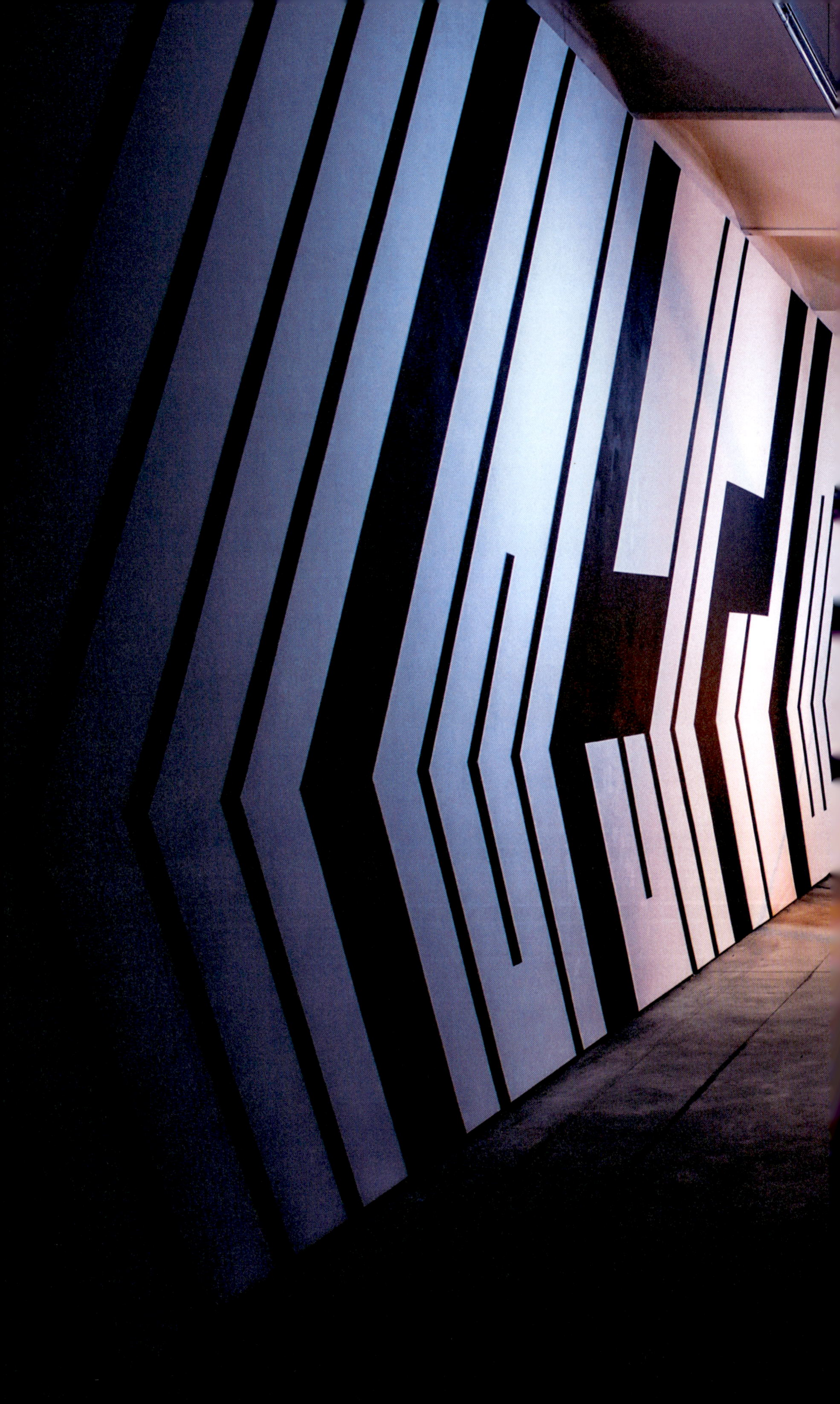

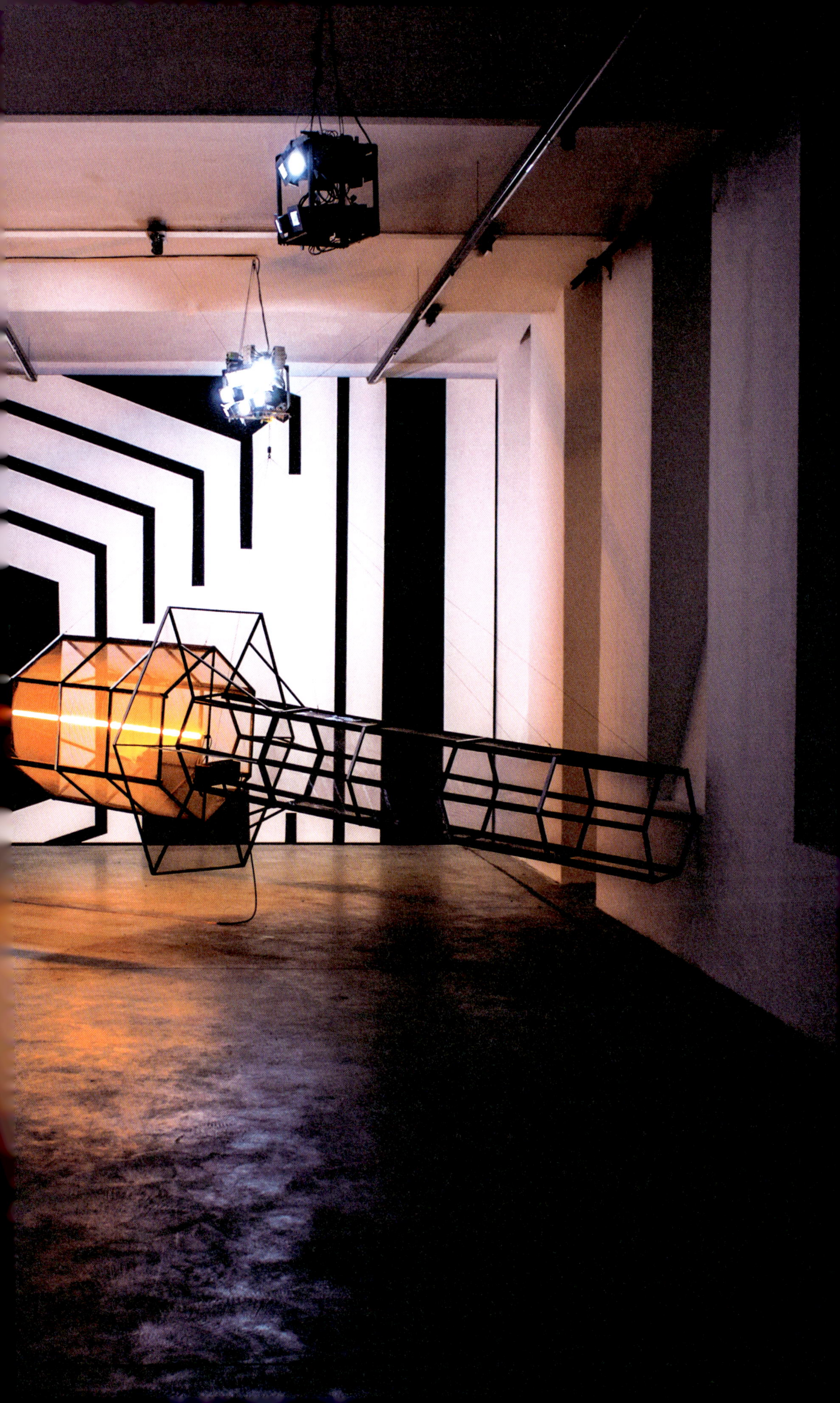

DYNAMIC ARTIFICIAL LIGHTING— THE LIGHTING "SCRIPT"

While in our previous experimental setups we programmed the light settings with the static values measured at the individual referenced museums, we now deployed variable light settings. By doing so, the range of variation between the highest and the lowest values measured at each respective museum was now emulated by the gallery's dynamic lighting. This made it clear that whenever we attend an actual exhibition, we are exposed to a variety of static lighting scenarios. At this point, I could now understand that lighting cannot be represented as an immutable museum standard. While the lighting ranged between 2,900 K and 3,500 K at the Museum of Applied Arts (MAK), it underwent a broader, more dynamic range between 4,040 K and 7,000 K at the Belvedere 21 setting (see table 14), because the latter's windows permit daylight to enter sideways.

LIGHT SETTING SCENE 1–13

```
<Scene remark=„KHM - 2900K">
<Setting cct=„2700" brightness=„178" endpoint=„11" />
<Setting cct=„2700" brightness=„178" endpoint=„12" />
<Setting cct=„2700" brightness=„178" endpoint=„14" />
</Scene>
```

```
<Scene remark=„MAK - 2900K / 3500K">
<Setting cct=„2900" brightness=„255" endpoint=„11" />
<Setting cct=„3300" brightness=„255" endpoint=„12" />
<Setting cct=„3500" brightness=„255" endpoint=„14" />
</Scene>
```

```
<Scene remark=„MQ - 2900K / 3700K">
<Setting cct=„3700" endpoint=„11" />
<Setting cct=„2900" endpoint=„12" />
<Setting cct=„3300" endpoint=„14" />
</Scene>
```

```
<Scene remark=„Belvedere21 - 2950K / 7000K">
<Setting cct=„4400" endpoint=„11" />
<Setting cct=„2950" endpoint=„12" />
<Setting cct=„7000" endpoint=„14" />
</Scene>
```

```
<Scene remark=„Secession - 4500K / 10000K">
<Setting cct=„5000" endpoint=„11" />
<Setting cct=„4500" endpoint=„12" />
<Setting cct=„10000" endpoint=„14" />
</Scene>
```

```
<Scene remark=„Lentos - 2900K / 9400K">
<Setting cct=„2900" endpoint=„11" />
<Setting cct=„4090" endpoint=„12" />
<Setting cct=„9400" endpoint=„14" />
</Scene>
```

```
<Scene remark=„Kunstforum - 2900K / 3500K">
<Setting cct=„3000" brightness=„100" endpoint=„11" />
<Setting cct=„2900" brightness=„100" endpoint=„12" />
<Setting cct=„3500" brightness=„100" endpoint=„14" />
</Scene>
```

```
<Scene remark=„Leopold - 2900K / 4000K">
<Setting cct=„4000" endpoint=„11" />
<Setting cct=„2900" endpoint=„12" />
<Setting cct=„9700" endpoint=„14" />
</Scene>
```

```
<Scene remark=„Rainermuseum - 2500K / 10000K">
<Setting cct=„5000" brightness=„255" endpoint=„11" />
<Setting cct=„2500" brightness=„255" endpoint=„12" />
<Setting cct=„10000" brightness=„255" endpoint=„14" />
</Scene>
```

```
<Scene remark=„Belvedere - 2900K / 5600K">
<Setting cct=„2900" endpoint=„11" />
<Setting cct=„3550" endpoint=„12" />
<Setting cct=„5600" endpoint=„14" />
</Scene>
```

```
<Scene remark=„Ferdinandeum - 2950K / 5300K">
<Setting cct=„3300" endpoint=„11" />
<Setting cct=„2950" endpoint=„12" />
<Setting cct=„5300" endpoint=„14" />
</Scene>
```

```
<Scene remark=„KunsthalleMQ - 2750K / 3300K">
<Setting cct=„3000" endpoint=„11" />
<Setting cct=„2750" endpoint=„12" />
<Setting cct=„3300" endpoint=„14" />
</Scene>
```

```
<Scene remark=„Albertina - 3000K / 4000K">
<Setting cct=„3000" endpoint=„11" />
<Setting cct=„3500" endpoint=„12" />
<Setting cct=„4000" endpoint=„14" />
</Scene>
```

△ Table 14. Programming code for Lightcubes 01 & 02: lighting script for *Lighthouse* exhibition

Interestingly, despite the sometimes quite high degrees of fluctuation, the transitions between light settings appeared very smooth. By targeting the color temperatures along Planck's curve, the dynamic lighting was perceived as very pleasant, even though the light settings changed in short intervals. One could observe that the audience was slow to become aware of the lighting changes in the exhibition space. As opposed to other comparable room installations where the luminous color vacillates and the effect lighting makes a viewer experience the change palpably, here one encountered a relatively sensorial experience with the deployment of lighting moods that emulate all facets of natural light. The viewer was only subtly aware that the lighting was changing in so many ways within a span of three minutes and 33 seconds. On average, visitors remained in the exhibition space between 14 and 20 minutes, so they experienced the complete lighting-script cycle four to six times. Typically, after the third time through, the viewer began to perceive all the nuances of the lighting script and witnessed the dynamic transformation of the exhibition space under the shifting light. Unlike with the previous experiments, the visitor no longer could select the gallery's light settings autonomously, but passively experienced the dynamic lighting of the artwork displayed in the center of the room. The lighting established a pattern of relationships between the artwork and the exhibition space, in which the audience participated.

Did this experiment succeed in establishing the sensual qualities of exhibition lighting, in terms of *object-oriented ontology*? Did it bring the audience closer to understanding this concept? Could we make the *ontology of light* understood inside a White Cube? We used dynamic illuminants to express the nature and essence of light, creating a synergy between the exhibition space, the art and the viewer. Light not only became a unifying element and a mediator, but it also appeared as a stand-alone object with its own real and sensual properties. The *Lighthouse* experiment expanded our understanding of exhibition lighting and demonstrated its creative and mediating potential as the nexus of art, space and viewer. The experiment raised the viewer's awareness of lighting as a tool for the artist. We were able to see how dynamic lighting interacted with art, how it affected the viewing of art, and what potential uses this could have for art in the future.

EPILOGUE

The prevailing lighting conditions at a museum can make or break the artwork that is exhibited. Certain artworks are not attuned to prevailing exhibition lighting conditions, and this can be a deciding factor as to whether or not an artwork is displayed. Is it not the museum's duty to create an appropriate setting for art, regardless of what period or stylistic movement it was created in? To do so, museum lighting should not subordinate the art, but rather support it. Dynamic lighting technologies could be used to tailor the lighting according to each museum's requirements. To accomplish this, we need to grasp the role of lighting within the pattern of relationships existing between the exhibition space, the art and the audience. In short, by using dynamic artificial light sources, any art is suitable for any space, and any space is suitable for any art.

Has the time not come to replace existing static artificial lighting with dynamic artificial lighting in exhibition spaces? The deployment of dynamic lighting technology within exhibition spaces requires that it conforms to the technical requirements of museum lighting. The implementation could be accomplished piecemeal, in consideration of the differentiation of ambient lighting and the targeted spotlighting of the artworks.

Nowadays, we typically deploy ceiling lamps and/or wall washers for ambient lighting and museum-grade spotlights for targeting specific artworks. This would also be possible by retrofitting existing fixtures with dynamic illuminants.

In existing exhibition spaces, the first step could be to replace the ceiling luminaires and wall washers in order to create ambient lighting that emulates natural daylight. This would be especially effective in museums such as Vienna's Kunsthistorisches Museum, where the original architectural design incorporated skylights. Thus, as a start, dynamic illuminants simulating daylight could replace all static artificial lights which were installed in the skylights that, for conservation purposes, had blocked out natural lighting. In this way, the original intent of the museum's architecture would be restored.

In the next step, artificially generated daylight could suffuse exhibition spaces such as Vienna's mumok and Salzburg's Museum der Moderne by retrofitting all recessed ceiling lamps with dynamic illuminants. This would yield a meaningful change of the atmosphere of the rooms and improve the visitor experience. It would remain incumbent upon experts to determine suitable preset dynamic light settings, whether they are adapted to the current course of daylight or specifically oriented to the exhibition design.

It could also be determined that the audience should view the artwork exclusively under a specific lighting mood, such as sunrise. Here, too, the potential of dynamic illuminants could be maximized to artificially emulate a specific period of the day, depending on the exhibition concept. A targeted implementation of artificial daylight in exhibition spaces would also counteract the stark contrasts between natural and artificial light that currently prevails in many museums, particularly where a building's exhibition spaces are artificially illuminated and circulation areas are naturally lit. *With* such a dynamic lighting juxtaposition, however, exhibition designers can more accurately carry out visual testing.

Such plainly visible contrasts have a negative impact on our apprehension of space. We easily perceive not only contrasting light intensities, but also differences in color rendering (CRI values) that impact the overall quality of lighting, especially when viewing color-intensive artworks. Without using a spectrometer, we can sense the difference between warm and cool white light with our naked eye, especially when they are juxtaposed. For example, if a work of art is illuminated at first by an illuminant with a CRI of 80 and in the second pass with a CRI of 90, we notice how differently the colors of the artwork appear. If such a juxtaposition is not possible, it becomes much more difficult to determine which light setting is most effective for a specific work of art.

While the subsequent experiments allowed the test subject to autonomously select one of several light-setting options, they were not given an initial reference setting to compare them to. Our research concept focused on how to use light as an interactive design tool for the exhibition space, and was primarily concerned with how the test subjects would deploy it autonomously. When we enter a space, we become choreographers who determine how and in what form we occupy the space. We step into the implied pattern of relationships and become active participants as well.

Our eyes adapt quite quickly to changes in light settings. When we visit a museum on a bright, sunny afternoon, our eyes rapidly adjust to a change in illuminance from 7,500 lux outside to an interior gallery illuminated as low as 50 lux. Our first impression of the exhibition space is that it is a gloomy atmosphere, but within a few minutes our eyes adjust and can appreciate the artwork in its full splendor.

Even if our research results were inconclusive regarding how different lighting conditions affect our judgement of art, we do associate a certain atmosphere with the exhibition spaces in question. I attribute this sensation to the space's lighting. The use of dynamic artificial illuminants has shown us that changes in lighting impact not only visual perception, but also nonvisual perception of light (see pages 68–71). Accordingly, lighting, and especially dynamic lighting, is said to produce a certain healthier, more positive mood. To prove this empirically would require test subjects to dwell much longer in an exhibition space, with a control group exposed to only static lighting. Neither condition was met in our experiments, thus further research is warranted.

Because of the disparate results of our research, we cannot develop empirically based, universal guidelines for planning the implementation of the material light. Even though we could not meet this goal, we were able to clearly foresee a potential for dynamic artificial illuminants within exhibition spaces. They allow us, as designers, to directly and interactively influence the patterns of relationships, taking into account the sensual and real perception of space. Light as a material is a design tool that impacts both our visual and nonvisual experience of space, and establishes the overall atmosphere of the space.

APPENDIX

STANDARDS AND GUIDELINES

ICOM Austria
Austrian national committee of the International Council of Museums

DIN 5035
Guidelines for artificial lighting issued by the German Institute for Standards (DIN)

DIN EN 12665
Basic terms and criteria for specifying lighting and illumination requirements issued by the German Institute for Standards (DIN)

DIN EN 13032-2
Guidelines for measurement and presentation of photometric data of lamps and luminaires, Part 2: Presentation of data for indoor and outdoor workplaces, issued by the German Institute for Standards (DIN)

DIN SPEC 5031-100
German Institute for Standards (DIN) guidelines for: Optical radiation physics and illuminating engineering, Part 100: Melanopic effects of ocular light on human beings—Quantities, symbols and action spectra

Institut für Museumsforschung
Standards issued by the Museum Research Institute of the State Museums of Berlin, Germany

CIE International Standards
issued by the CIE (International Commission on Illumination)

ÖNORM EN 12464-1 / *EN 12464-1*
Austrian and German standards for light and lighting—lighting of work places—Part 1: Indoor work places (Edition 2021-12-15)

CIE 157:2004
Guidelines for controlling damage to museum objects by optical radiation, issued by the CIE (International Commission on Illumination)

GLA (Global Lighting Association)
Application of CIE 13.3-1995 with Associated CRI-based Colour Rendition Properties, December 2018

GLOSSARY OF TERMS AND ABBREVIATIONS

Sources: *electropedia.org, **lrc.rpi.edu, ***wikipedia.org

TERM / ABBREVIATION	DEFINITION
Blackbody radiator*	See Planckian radiator
BMP	Bitmap
CCT**	Correlated Color tTemperature (measured in Kelvin)
CIE	International Commission on Illumination (defines lighting standards)
Correlated color temperature**	Measure of light source color appearance defined by the proximity of the light source's chromaticity coordinates to the blackbody locus (measured in Kelvin)
CRI***	Color Rendering Index (CRI) CRI is a quantitative measure of the ability of a light source to reveal the colors of various objects faithfully in comparison with a natural or standard light source. The highest possible value of 100 Ra is given to a light source whose spectrum is identical to the spectrum of daylight
Dynamic (artificial) lighting	In the context of lighting, "dynamic" describes lighting that varies over a given period of time as a result of regulating one or more of its parameters—for example, its intensity, luminous color or direction
E **or** E_v	Symbol for illuminance (lux)
$\bar{E}_m$	Illuminance maintenance value—value below which the illuminance level must not fall in the visual task area.
HCL	Human Centric Lighting
I **or** I_v	Symbol for luminous intensity
Illuminance*	Density of incident luminous flux with respect to area at a point on a real or imaginary surface measured in lux (symbol E or E_v)
K	Kelvin (unit of color temperature)
KHM	Kunsthistorisches Museum (Museum of Art History in Vienna, Austria)

TERM / ABBREVIATION	DEFINITION
LED	Light-emitting diode
Luminaire*	Apparatus which distributes, filters or transforms the light transmitted from at least one source of optical radiation and which includes, except the sources themselves, all the parts necessary for fixing and protecting the sources and, where necessary, circuit auxiliaries together with the means for connecting them to the power supply
Luminous color*	Color perceived to belong to an area that appears to be emitting light as a primary light source, or that appears to be specularly reflecting such light
Luminous intensity*	Density of luminous flux with respect to solid angle in a specified direction (symbol: I_v or I)
lx or lux	Lux (unit of illuminance)
mumok	Museum moderner Kunst Stiftung Ludwig Wien (Museum of Modern and Contemporary Art in Vienna, Austria)
Object-oriented ontology (OOO)***	A 21st-century school of metaphysical thought that rejects the privileging of human existence over the existence of nonhuman objects. Object-oriented ontology maintains that objects exist independently of human perception and are not ontologically exhausted by their relations with humans or other objects
OOO	See object-oriented ontology
Planck's law*	Law giving the spectral distribution of radiance of a Planckian radiator as a function of wavelength and temperature
Planckian radiator*/ Blackbody*	Ideal thermal radiator that absorbs completely all incident radiation, whatever the wavelength, the direction of incidence or the polarization. A Planckian radiator has, for any wavelength and any direction, the maximum spectral distribution of radiance for a thermal radiator in thermal equilibrium at a given temperature
R_a	Symbol for Color Rendering Index (CRI)
RGB	Red, green, blue (additive primary colors)
R_{UGL}	The Unified Glare Rating (UGR) glare value according to the internationally standardized method (CIE 117:1995) for describing discomfort glare
UGR	Unified Glare Rating, a procedure for the evaluation of discomfort glare from artificial lighting in indoor spaces
U_O*	Luminance uniformity, quotient of minimum luminance and average luminance of a surface.

BIBLIOGRAPHY

Adelson, E.H. (2000). "Lightness Perception and Lightness Illusion," in *The New Cognitive Neurosciences*, 2nd ed., M. Gazzaniga, ed., Cambridge, MA: MIT Press, pp. 339–351

Arnheim, R. (1965). *Kunst und Sehen : Eine Psychologie des schöpferischen Auge*, Berlin, Boston: De Gruyter

Bachmann, U. (2006). *Farben zwischen Licht und Dunkelheit / Colours between Light and Darkness*, Sulgen/ Zürich: Verlag Niggli AG

Bartenbach, C. (2009). *Handbuch für Lichtgestaltung*, Vienna et al.: Springer

Becker, P. (2009). *In der Bewusstseinsfalle? Geist und Gehirn in der Diskussion von Theologie, Philosophie und Naturwissenschaften*, Göttingen: Vandenhoeck & Ruprecht GmbH, p. 54

Benitez-Quiroz, C.F., Srinivasan, R., Martinez, A.M. (2018). "Facial color is an efficient mechanism to visually transmit emotion," *Proceedings of the National Academy of Sciences*, 115(14), pp. 3581–3586

Berson, D.M, Dunn, F.A,, Takao, M. (2002). "Phototransduction by Retinal Ganglion Cells That Set the Circadian Clock," *Science*, 8 February 2002, Vol. 295, Issue 5557, pp. 1070–1073

Brown, M. (2018). "Fine Art Society sale to include works by Whistler, Gluck and Peter Blake," *The Guardian*, retrieved 9 December 2018

Böhme, G. (2006). *Architektur und Atmosphäre*, Munich: Fink

Bollnow, O.F. (1963). *Mensch und Raum*, 8th edition, Stuttgart: Verlag W. Kohlhammer GmbH

Bollnow, O.F. (1963) *Human space*, trans. by Christine Shuttleworth (2011), London: Hyphen Press

Boyce, P.R. (2014) *Human Factors in Lighting*, 3rd edition, Boca Raton: CRC Press

Cabañas, K.M. (2008). "Yves Klein's Performative Realism," in *Grey Room*, No. 31, Cambridge: The MIT Press, pp. 6–31

Choi, K., Shin, C., Kim, T., Chung, H.J., Suk, H.J. (2019). "Awakening effects of blue-enriched morning light exposure on university students' physiological and subjective responses," *Scientific Reports*, 9(1), p. 345

Davidson, S., Rylands, P., Bogner, D., et al. (2004). *Peggy Guggenheim & Frederick Kiesler: The Story of Art of This Century*, Fondazione Peggy Guggenheim, Ostfildern-Ruit: Hatje Cantz; New York, NY: D.A.P.

Davis, R.G. & Ginthner, D.N. (1990). "Correlated Color Temperature, Illuminance Level, and the Kruithof Curve," *Journal of the Illuminating Engineering Society*, 19:1, pp. 27–38

Doppler, S. (2012). *Die Funktion in der zeitgenössischen Museumsarchitektur*, Diploma thesis, Universität Wien, Historisch-Kulturwissenschaftliche Fakultät, Advisor: Kitlitschka, W.

Fairchild, M. D., & Reniff, L. (1995). "Time course of chromatic adaptation for color-appearance judgments," *Journal of the Optical Society of America, A, Optics, Image Science & Vision,* 12(5), pp. 824–833

Feltrin, F., Hanselaer, P., Leccese, F., Smet, K. (2017). "Analysis of painted artworks' color appearance under various lighting settings," *2017 IEEE International Conference on Environment and Electrical Engineering and 2017 IEEE Industrial and Commercial Power Systems Europe (EEEIC / I&CPS Europe)*, Milan, Italy, 2017, pp. 1–6

Feltrin, F., Leccese, F., Hanselaer, P., Smet, K. (2020). "Impact of Illumination Correlated Color Temperature, Background Lightness, and Painting Color Content on Color Appearance and Appreciation of Paintings." *LEUKOS*, 16:1, pp. 25–44

Fischer, E.P., (2006). "Naturwissenschaftliches zu den Taten des Lichts – A scientific view of the deeds of light" in Bachmann, U. (2006), *Farben zwischen Licht und Dunkelheit / Colours between Light and Darkness*, Sulgen/Zürich: Verlag Niggli AG

Garside, D., Curran, K., Korenberg, C., MacDonald, L., Teunissen, K., Robson, S. (2017). "How is museum lighting selected? An insight into current practice in UK museums," *Journal of the Institute of Conservation*, 40:1, pp. 3–14

Gilbert, P., Haeberli, W. (2008). *Physics in the arts*, 1st ed., Burlington, MA et. al.: Elsevier Acad. Press

Graser, A., Hötzl, M. (2016). "Architektur aus Licht," *Architektur & Bauforum*, Ausgabe 04/2016, Vienna: Österreichischer Wirtschaftsverlag GmbH, pp. 4–5

Gregory, R.L. (2015,). *Eye and Brain: The Psychology of Seeing – Fifth Edition,* REV-Revised, 5. Princeton University Press

Haarmann, H. (2005). *Schwarz: Eine kleine Kulturgeschichte*, Frankfurt am Main: Peter Lang Europäischer Verlag der Wissenschaften

Harman, G. (2018). *Object-Oriented Ontology: A New Theory of Everything*, London: Pelican Books

Haun, M. (2002). "Objektorientierte Ontologie," in: *Handbuch Wissensmanagement,* Berlin, Heidelberg: Springer, pp. 347–365

Heilmann, R. (2013). *Licht: Die faszinierende Geschichte eines Phänomens*, Munich: F.A. Herbig Verlagsbuchhandlung GmbH

Hertog, W., Llenas, A., Carreras, J. (2015). "Optimizing indoor illumination quality and energy efficiency using a spectrally tunable lighting system to augment natural daylight," *Optics Express* 23, A1564–A1574

Hurlbert, A., Cuttle, C. (2020). "New Museum Lighting for People and Paintings," *LEUKOS*, 16:1, pp. 1–5

Hurlbert, A., Pearce, B. Aston, S. (2016). "Tuning Light to See and Feel Better: the Human Visual and Non-Visual Responses to Spectral Variations in Light," in conference proceedings, CIE 2016 Lighting Quality and Energy Efficiency Conference, Newcastle [UK] University Library

Karasov, D. (1995). "Tools of Vision," *Public Art Review*, Vol. 7, No. 1, 1995, p. 13

Kesner, C.W, (1993). "Museum Exhibition Lighting: Visitor Needs and Perceptions of Quality," *Journal of the Illuminating Engineering Society*, 22:1, pp. 45–54

Kiesler, F. (1942). Press release pertaining to the "Architectural Aspects of the Gallery," published in Davidson, S., Rylands, P., Bogner, D., et.al. (2004). *Peggy Guggenheim & Frederick Kiesler: The Story of Art of This Century*, Fondazione Peggy Guggenheim, Ostfildern-Ruit: Hatje Cantz ; New York, NY : D.A.P., pp. 176ff.

Kiesler, F. (1943). "New Display Techniques for Art of This Century," *Architectural Forum*, 78/2, February 1943, pp. 49–50

Kiesler, F. (1966). *Inside the Endless House: Art, People, and Architecture: a Journal*, New York, NY: Simon and Schuster

Kries, Mateo (2013). *3 Lightopia Design-Museum*, Berlin: Visionen. Vitra Design Museum, Weil am Rhein

Küppers, H. (1981). *Die Logik der Farbe: Theoretische Grundlage der Farbenlehre*, 2nd ed., Munich: Verlag Georg D.W. Callwey

Lam, W.M.C. (1977). *Perception and Lighting as Formgivers for Architecture,* New York (NY): McGraw-Hill

Lehrer, J. (2010). *Prousts Madeleine: Hirnforschung für Kreative.* Munich, Zürich: Piper

Leydecker, S. (2013). *Innenräume entwerfen*, Basel: Birkhäuser

Llenas, A., Carerras, J. (2018). "Enhancing comfort, alertness and productivity in indoor working environments using dynamic multi-channel LED lighting systems that mimic daylight," in proceedings of CIE 2018 "Topical Conference on Smart Lighting," Taipei, ROC

Llenas, A., Carreras, J. (2019). "Spectrally tunable LED light engines and the metamer optimization tool (MOTO)," in proceedings of SPIE 10940, Light-Emitting Devices, Materials, and Applications, 109401L

Llenas, A., Hurlbert, A., Lam, F., Manudhane, R., Gupta, G., Giddings, J., Carreras, J. (2019). "Testing the use of spectrally tunable lighting systems to improve comfort, alertness and sleep quality in indoor working environment," in proceedings of the 29th CIE, Washington D.C., pp. 830–837

Mack, G. (1999). *Kunstmuseen: Auf den Weg ins 21. Jahrhundert*, Basel: Birkhäuser Verlag für Architektur

McColl, Shelley L. and JA Veitch (2001). "Full-spectrum fluorescent lighting: a review of its effects on physiology and health," *Psychological Medicine* 31, pp. 949–964

Mönninger, M. (2010). *Coop Himmelb(l)au—Complete Works 1968–2010*, Cologne: Taschen

Nänni, J. (2008). *Visuelle Wahrnehmung*, Sulgen: Niggli

Naredi-Rainer, P., Hilger, O. (2004). *Entwurfsatlas Museumsbau, Basel:* Birkhäuser

Nascimento, SM., Masuda, O. (2014). "Best lighting for visual appreciation of artistic paintings—Experiments with real paintings and real illumination," *J. Opt. Soc. Am.* Vol. 31, pp. A214–A219

Noever, P. (2002). *James Turrell: The Other Horizon,* Ostfildern-Ruit: Hatje Cantz

O'Doherty, B. (1976, 1986). *Inside the White Cube: The Ideology of the Gallery Space*, San Francisco, CA: The Lapis Press

Pelowski, M., Foster, M., Tinio, P., Scholl, M., Leder, H. (2017). "Beyond the Lab: An Examination of Key Factors Influencing Interaction with 'Real' and Museum-based Art," *Psychology of Aesthetics Creativity and the Arts*, 11(3), pp. 245–264

Pelowski, M., Graser, A., Specker, E., Forster, M., von Hinüber, J., Leder, H. (2019). "Does Gallery Lighting Really Have an Impact on Appreciation of Art? An Ecologically Valid Study of Lighting Changes and the Assessment and Emotional Experience With Representational and Abstract Paintings," *Frontiers in Psychology*, Vol. 10, Article 2148

Pinto, P.D., Linhares, J.M.M., Nascimento, S.M.C. (2008). "Correlated color temperature preferred by observers for illumination of artistic paintings." *J. Opt. Soc. Am. A Opt. Image Sci. Vis.* 25, pp. 623–630.

Pridmore, R. W. (2017). "Preferred illumination for paintings: Cool-warm balanced colour temperature predicted from radiometry and colorimetry," *Lighting Research & Technology*, 49(5), pp. 618–631

Ris, H.R. (2019) *Beleuchtungstechnik für Praktiker*, 6th ed., Berlin: VDE Verlag

Saleh, B.E. (2008). *Grundlagen der Photonik*, Weinheim: Wiley-VCH, pp. 75ff.

Schanda, J., Csuti, P., Szabo, F. (2016). "A New Concept of Color Fidelity for Museum Lighting," *LEUKOS*, 12:1-2, pp. 71–77

Schielke, T. (2020). "Interpreting Art with Light: Museum Lighting between Objectivity and Hyperrealism," *LEUKOS*, 16:1, pp. 7–24

Schöne, W. (1989). *Über das Licht in der Malerei*, Berlin: Mann

Schürmann, E. (2000). *Erscheinen und Wahrnehmen: Eine vergleichende Studie zur Kunst von James Turrell und der Philosophie Merleau-Pontys*, Munich: Fink

Schwarz, M., (1997). *Licht, Farbe, Raum. Künstlerisch-wissenschaftliches Symposium*, Braunschweig: Verlag Leporello

Schwarz, M., (1998). *Licht und Raum. Elektrisches Licht in der Kunst des 20. Jahrunderts*, Cologne: Wienand

Scuello, M., Abramov, I., Gordon, J., Weintraub, S. (2004b). "Museum lighting: Optimizing the illuminant," *Color Research & Application*, 29, pp. 121–127

Scuello, M., Abramov, I., Gordon, J., & Weintraub, S. (2004). "Museum lighting: Why are some illuminants preferred?" *J. Opt. Soc. Am. A* 21(2), pp. 306–311

Spitschan, M. (2019). "Melanopsin contributions to non-visual and visual function," *Current Opinion in Behavioral Sciences*, Vol. 30, pp. 67–72

Stromer, K., Fischer E.P. (2006). *Die Natur der Farbe*, Cologne: DuMont

Tate (2018). "White cube, Art Term," https://www.tate.org.uk/art/art-terms/w/white-cube, retrieved 25 November 2018

Thomson, G. (1986). *The Museum Environment*, 2nd ed., Butterworth-Heinemann Series in Conservation and Museology

Tuchman, M. (1971). *A Report on the Art and Technology Program of the Los Angeles County Museum of Art, 1967–1971.* New York: Viking

Ulmann, P.P. (2015). *Licht und Beleuchtung: Handbuch und Planungshilfe,* Berlin: DOM publishers

Verjux, M. (1993). *Michel Verjux* (exhibition catalogue), Westfälischer Kunstverein Münster (publ.), Stuttgart: Verlag Cantz

Verma, R.L. (1969). *Al-Hazen: father of modern optics,* Al-Arabi

Würtinger, W. (2011). "Arkadien und angenehme Feinde. Die Bildhauerateliers im Prater," in Boeckl, M., *Generalprobe für die Ringstraße*, Vereinigung Bildender KünstlerInnen Wiener Secession, Berlin: Revolver Publishing, pp. 152ff.

Zajonc, A. (1993). *Catching the light: The Entwined History of Light and Mind,* New York: Oxford University Press

Zajonc, A. (1994). *Die gemeinsame Geschichte von Licht und Bewußtsein*, trans. by Kober, H., Reinbeck bei Hamburg: Rowohlt Verlag GmbH

Zhai Q, Luo M, Liu X., (2015). "The impact of illuminance and colour temperature on viewing fine art paintings under LED lighting," *Lighting Research & Technology*, 47(7), pp. 795–809

Zhai Q., Luo M., Liu X., (2016). "The impact of LED lighting parameters on viewing fine art paintings," *Lighting Research & Technology*, 48(6), pp. 711–725

Zwimpfer, M. (2012). *Licht und Farbe: Physik Erscheinung Wahrnehmung*, Sulgen et al.: Niggli

BIOGRAPHIES

Author, Artist, Translator, Graphic Designer

ANDREA GRASER

Andrea Graser (b. 1976) is an architect specializing in lighting. In 2014, she founded the architecture and lighting design firm Studio Okular (studio-okular.com) in Vienna, Austria. She earned her PhD in technical sciences from the Institute of Architecture at the University of Applied Arts Vienna. From 2001 until 2014 she was a project partner of Wolf D. Prix at Coop Himmelb(l)au, where she led the design and planning process for award-winning international museum projects and cultural buildings. For over 20 years, she has explored the material of light in art and architecture.

FRIEDRICH BIEDERMANN

Friedrich Biedermann (b. 1975) is an artist based in Vienna, Austria. His sculptures, installations and paintings explore the ontology of light. After studying sculpture at the University of Applied Arts Vienna, in 2002 he remained there to work with Brigitte Kowanz as an assistant and adjunct lecturer at the Institute of Transmedia Art. Since 2008, he has been a freelance artist (friedrichbiedermann.com). His art has been presented in numerous international exhibitions and architectural projects.

MICHAEL BERNSTEIN

US-American expat Michael Bernstein has lived in Vienna, Austria, since 2001. Currently a freelance writer, editor and translator for print and digital media, Bernstein was previously the Administrator for The Phillips Collection (a museum of Modern Art in Washington, D.C.) and for the New York Foundation for the Arts. (www.michaelbernstein.contently.com)

CAROLINE ECKER

Caroline Ecker is a crossmedia graphic and product designer, based in Vienna and Wald am Arlberg, Austria. She was trained in natural sciences, philosophy, arts, architecture and design. In 2015 she founded her studio (www.ce-design.org), currently focusing on editorial and corporate design in the digital and analog world.

ACKNOWLEDGMENTS

A part of this book stemmed from our participation in Frankfurt am Main's Luminale light festival nearly six years ago, when we exhibited our installation entitled *Light Path*. It was there I met my former structural engineering professor, Prof. Klaus Bollinger, who then headed the Institute of Architecture at the University of Applied Arts Vienna. His interest was piqued as he observed our walk-through installation with a handheld spectrometer. Our ensuing conversations and discussions provided the initial impetus for this book. Thus, my foremost thanks go to Prof. Bollinger, my PhD advisor, for his support from the initial field study throughout the research and completion of this book. Further thanks go to the University of Applied Arts Vienna and my colleagues at the Institute of Architecture (I oA) who supported me during the process. Special thanks also go to Dr. Gerald Bast, Rector of the University of Applied Arts Vienna, who provided me with significant support in many ways, including locating suitable research premises.

I would like to express my gratitude to all of my research partners for their support and cooperation: Prof. Günther Leising at the Graz University of Technology and Dr. Stefan Tasch for providing their scientific and technical support, as well as infrastructure during the planning and execution of the experiments; Prof. Helmut Leder and his colleagues at EVA Labs; and especially Matthew Pelowski, Eva Specker, Michael Forster and Josefine von Hinüber at the University of Vienna, for their lively discourse and implementation of the empirical study.

I am grateful for the opportunity to share my thoughts and approaches to this book with the artist Friedrich Biedermann, who actively supported me in the implementation of my research projects and persistently motivated me throughout its completion. I also thank him for providing the *Spectrum 2016* series of pictures and for collaborating on the concept of the *Lighthouse* installation and sculpture, as well.

I would also like to thank all those who provided artwork for the exhibitions that enabled our research projects. Frauke Danner, Georg Eldbarb, Alina Kunitsyna and Bernd Oppl loaned their artwork for the exhibit *Five Artists × Five Museums*. The curator of University of Applied Arts Vienna, art historian Barbara Pflanzner, supported me in selecting three artworks from its collection and archive for the first series of tests.

Special thanks also go to Alexandra Graupner and her colleagues at the Angewandte Interdisciplinary Lab, who made it possible to carry out the research project within an actual public exhibition context. Thanks to all the museums and exhibition institutions that gave me the opportunity to measure their prevailing lighting conditions. I am eternally grateful for the numerous conversations I had with museum experts and museum employees while planning and implementing the measurement processes.

For this book specifically, I would like to thank the publisher—in particular, Katharina Holas for her thoughtful engagement—as well as Anja Seipenbusch-Hufschmied for her advice and support. But above all, my thanks go to Caroline Ecker, who developed and skillfully implemented the stunning and very harmonious graphic design concept with great finesse and sophistication. A special thank you goes to the translator Michael Bernstein, who diligently translated the German manuscript into English. His diligent contextual analysis of the text required precision and he finely honed several passages.

Last, but not least, I thank my family.

Imprint

Andrea Graser

Studio Okular, A-Vienna, www.studio-okular.com

Printed with the financial support of the University of Applied Arts Vienna

Project Management "Edition Angewandte" on behalf of the University of Applied Arts Vienna:
Anja Seipenbusch-Hufschmied, A-Vienna

Content and Production Editor on behalf of the Publisher:
Katharina Holas, A-Vienna

Translation from German into English and proofreading:
Michael Bernstein, A-Vienna

Layout, cover design, typography, and image editing:
Caroline Ecker, ce-design, A-Vienna / Wald a. A.

Printing: Holzhausen, the book-printing brand of Gerin Druck GmbH, A-Wolkersdorf
Paper: Sappi Raw 135 g/m², Koehler Eco Black 270 g/m²
Typeface: Avenir, Baskerville, Circe Slab A

Library of Congress Control Number: 2022947757

Bibliographic information published by the German National Library
The German National Library lists this publication in the Deutsche Nationalbibliografie; detailed bibliographic data are available on the Internet at http://dnb.dnb.de.

ISSN 1866-248X

ISBN 978-3-0356-2705-3

e-ISBN (PDF) 978-3-0356-2706-0

P.O. Box 44, 4009 Basel, Switzerland

Part of Walter de Gruyter GmbH, Berlin/Boston

MIX
Papier aus verantwortungsvollen Quellen
FSC® C108696

9 8 7 6 5 4 3 2 1 www.birkhauser.com